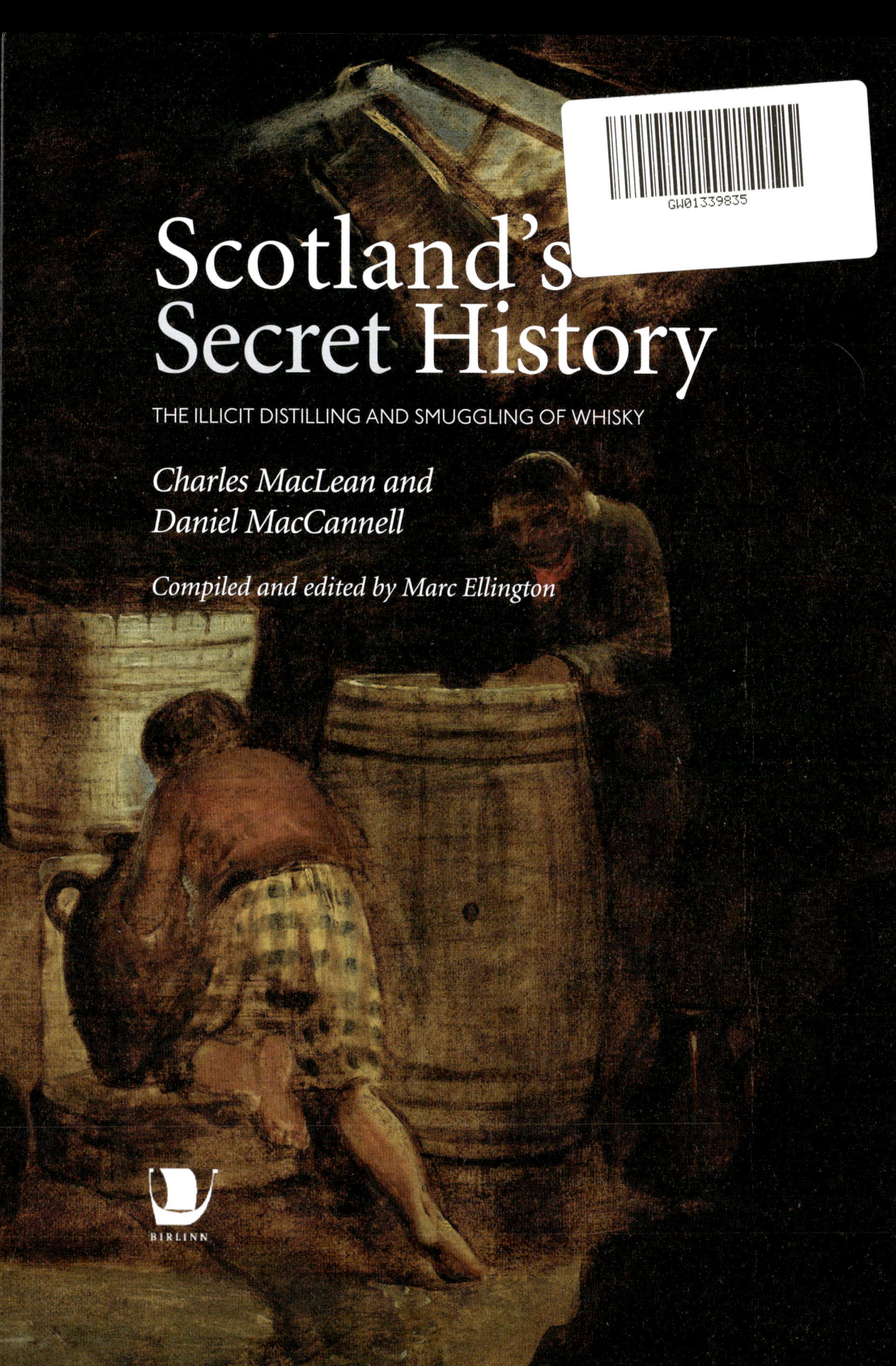

Scotland's Secret History

THE ILLICIT DISTILLING AND SMUGGLING OF WHISKY

Charles MacLean and
Daniel MacCannell

Compiled and edited by Marc Ellington

BIRLINN

First published in 2017 by
Birlinn Limited
West Newington House
10 Newington Road
Edinburgh
EH9 1QS

www.birlinn.co.uk

The Historic Roots of Illicit Distilling © Charles MacLean 2017
Smuggling's Heartland © Dan MacCannell 2017
Introduction © Marc Ellington 2017
Making Whisky © Denis McBain 2017
The Jacobite Legacy © Murray Pittock 2017
The Bard and the Bottle © David Purdie 2017
The Dram in Folklore © Tom McKean 2017
Bays, Beaches and Caves © David Ferguson 2017
Banff © Jay Wilson 2017
Scotland's Lost Distilleries © Brian Townsend 2017

All rights reserved.

No part of this publication may be reproduced, stored or transmitted
in any form without the express written permission of the publisher.

ISBN 978 1 78027 303 7 (paperback)
ISBN 978 1 78027 540 6 (hardback limited edition for William Grant & Sons)

British Library Cataloguing-in-Publication Data
A catalogue record for this book is available from the British Library

Designed by Mark Blackadder

Frontispiece: Painting of illicit distillers by Sir Edwin Landseer.

The Publisher gratefully acknowledges subsidy from

towards the publication of this book.

Printed and bound by TJ International

In memory of Charles Grant Gordon, 1927–2013, whose interest in his Cabrach heritage and the history of whisky-making in Scotland served as a continuing source of inspiration to those involved in producing this book.

Contents

Introduction   ix
    Marc Ellington

The Historic Roots of Illicit Distilling and Smuggling in Scotland   1
    Charles MacLean
      I   A Nation of Smugglers   2
      II   Union and Disorder   9
      III   Ancient Liberties   12
      IV   Open Transgression   19
      V   Distilling in a Thousand Hands   31
      VI   Carrot and Stick   51
      VII   The Last Gasps   63

Smuggling's Heartland: The Cabrach   73
    Daniel MacCannell
      I   A Raiding Base on the Highland Line   75
      II   Nursery of the Royalist Cavalry   83
      III   The Campbells Triumphant and the Coming of Smuggling   85
      IV   Resistance Continues: The Ferintosh Years   90
      V   A Logic of Its Own: From Smuggling to Distilling, 1760 to 1790   100
      VI   After the Ferintosh: Cabrach Smuggling's Golden Age   103
      VII   Passing into History?   114

Features
    Making Whisky   7
      Dennis McBain
    The Jacobite Legacy   16
      Murray Pittock
    The Bard and the Bottle   47
      David Purdie
    The Dram in Folklore   67
      Tom McKean

Opposite.
Tussle for the Keg,
John Pettie (1839–93).

Bays, Beaches and Caves: A Smuggler's Paradise	96
David Ferguson	
Banff: The Smuggler's Royal Burgh	109
Jay Wilson	
Scotland's Lost Distilleries	120
Brian Townsend	

Epilogue 125

Endnotes 131

Acknowledgements 140

Permissions 141

Index 143

Introduction
Marc Ellington

Bloody street battles, shocking levels of public corruption and cat-and-mouse chases across Highland hills: the story of illicit distilling and smuggling of whisky in Scotland is as full of excitement and intrigue as the most outlandish tales from the pens of the nation's fiction writers. Throughout history, outlaws, renegades and fugitives from justice have often captured the public imagination. Seldom, however, have the perceived perpetrators of any illegal activity become so firmly entrenched in a nation's culture and history as those in Scotland involved in illicit distilling and smuggling.

The culmination of one of the most extensive programmes of research and investigations on the subject to date, *Scotland's Secret History* combines detailed studies by Charles MacLean, an acknowledged world expert on Scotch whisky, and historian Daniel MacCannell, with contributions from a range of leading authorities and academics, which together serve to increase our knowledge and understanding of this highly important yet widely misunderstood aspect of Scotland's history and heritage.

While other books have dealt with the illegal drinks trade in the reign of Queen Anne and the small-scale smugglers who rose to prominence during the Napoleonic Wars, this is the first to directly confront and dispel a number of firmly established false assumptions concerning this clandestine activity. A substantial portion of the myths and legends that surround illicit distilling can be traced to Scotland's vast resource of traditional ballads, folk songs and poetry – further reinforced by the dramatic and often highly romanticised visual images created by eighteenth- and nineteenth-century artists such as Sir David Wilkie and Sir Edwin Landseer.

Central to dispelling these often deep-seated myths and incorrect perceptions is the revelation that illicit distilling and smuggling together formed an important economic activity in Scotland, which at its peak operated on a massive scale and for years was a valuable source of income for not only crofters, small-scale farmers and others scraping a subsistence living in remote areas of

An early seventeenth-century distilling operation, from *The Art of Distillation*, 1615.

the Highlands but also major landowners, merchants and civic authorities throughout the country.

As well as examining the process employed in making whisky and identifying the various locations where illicit distilling took place, the following pages provide important information concerning smuggling operations, the individuals involved and the extraordinary measures that were taken to avoid the unwelcome attention of those in authority – factions of which often benefited themselves from this vast illegal trade.

Interrelated Scottish families living as far apart as the Cabrach in Aberdeenshire, the Portuguese Atlantic island of Madeira, Xerez de la Frontera in Spain and Dunkirk in Flanders formed a vast international network involved in a rich mixture of illegal alcohol production, smuggling and not infrequently anti-Unionist and/or Jacobite conspiracy. Of critical importance is the role played by the small harbours and towns on the Moray Firth in the north-east of Scotland, as well as the larger ports of Aberdeen, Banff and Montrose.

In addition to revealing that illicit distilling and smuggling whisky were as much Scottish social, cultural and political phenomena as economic, the authors establish them in their rightful place as the historic predecessors to Scotland's present highly successful whisky industry.

While acknowledging illicit distilling and smuggling operations that took place in other locations throughout Scotland, the work focuses strongly on what occurred in the Cabrach – a remote, sparsely populated parish in upland

Introduction

Illicit distillers and their accomplices plying their trade.

Aberdeenshire which, throughout much of its history (along with its immediate neighbours in Glenlivet and Strathdon), was engaged in this clandestine activity to an extent and on a scale which it could be argued is without parallel elsewhere in Scotland.

The area was also home to a small group of closely interrelated families which for generations derived their livelihood, in part or in whole, from illicit distilling. It is, therefore, perhaps no coincidence that members of these self-same families have contributed greatly to the development of Scotland's highly successful whisky industry.

In shedding new light on an aspect of our history which has for long been shrouded in mystery, the following pages provide a valuable insight into the realities of the illegal distilling and smuggling of whisky in Scotland, as opposed to the confused, deep-seated and often fanciful representations that have dominated perceptions of this important element of Scotland's history and heritage.

And finally, as you embark upon the journey of discovery that awaits you, I would propose a toast of the good stuff to those men and women in Scotland whose labour has involved the making of whisky, both legal and illicit.

Here's to you!

Sláinte!

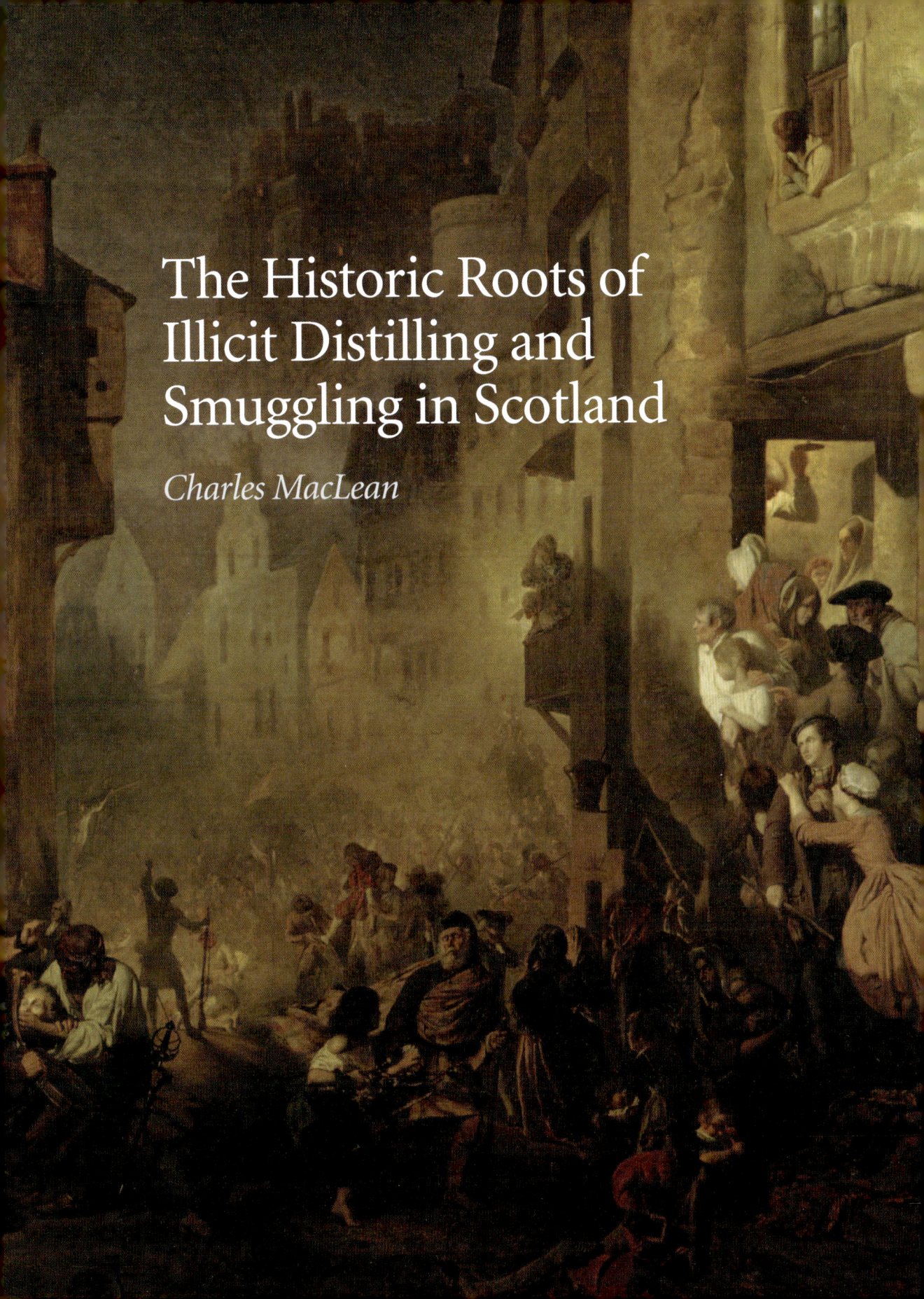

The Historic Roots of Illicit Distilling and Smuggling in Scotland

Charles MacLean

I
A Nation of Smugglers

'The Scots used to have a reputation overseas for being the one nation in the world who were compulsive smugglers. They acquired it long before 1707 [the Act of Union]'

The Smugglers, Duncan Fraser

The verb *schmuggelen* entered the English language from German in the late seventeenth century, although a related word in Old English, *smūgan* ('to creep'), is found to have been in use as early as the fourteenth century. In its strictest sense 'smuggling' simply means 'to import or export illegally, or to convey secretly'. In Scotland its meaning was immediately extended to describe, and has remained synonymous with, the activities of those who distilled whisky illegally.

'Illegal' in this context meant 'without taking out a licence to distil or paying excise duty (in the case of home-produced goods) or paying customs' tariffs (in the case of imported goods)'. As such, a smuggler could be an illicit distiller, the person who transported the contraband or the person who dealt with goods imported from abroad, without duty having been paid. And, in some cases, all three.

'Excise', 'excijs' or 'excyse' duty was first introduced by the Dutch in 1596 as a tax on domestically produced goods, especially alcohol. The idea of imposing such a tax in England was proposed to Charles I by his Treasurer, the Earl of Bedford. When Parliament got wind of the scheme, it complained in the Grand Remonstrance of 1641 of 'unjust and pernicious attempts to extort great payments from the subjects by way of excise'. Two years later, in September 1643, Parliament itself introduced what they had objected to so strongly in order to raise money to wage war against the king. The next year the Scottish parliament followed suit – to pay for the army of the Covenant.

The Excyse Act was passed on 31 January 1644. Among the 35 classes of goods to be taxed were spirits, at the rate of 2s 8d (Scots) (13p) per Scots pint (approximately 1.5 litres) on 'everie pynt of aquavytie or strong watteris sold within the country'.[1] The key word here is *sold*: the tax applied equally to both imported foreign and homemade spirits, but it only applied if the spirits were sold. Distilling for domestic consumption, from grains grown by a local community or a landowner, was perfectly legal until 1781.

In late 1655, during the Commonwealth established by Oliver Cromwell, duty was lowered to 2d per Scots quart; the following year Thomas Tucker, a

Oliver Cromwell, who, during the Commonwealth, fundamentally reorganised the system of customs and excise collection in Scotland.

Measuring gauge used by excisemen – hence the name 'gaugers', literally 'measurers'.

Cromwellian official, reorganised the collection of customs and excise duties in Scotland. It divided the country into 21 'precincts' or administrative districts, each of which was set a financial target. The top six by anticipated revenue were Fife and Kinross (£1,480), Edinburgh (£1,200), Glasgow (£1,000), 'Aberdeene and Bamff' (£980), 'Pearth' (£840) and 'Ayre' (£800). No revenue at all was expected from Argyll, Bute, Inverness-shire, Ross, Sutherland, Cromarty and Caithness.[2]

Following the Restoration of Charles II in 1660, duty was again reduced, to 'one peny ... for every gallon of Strong Water or Aqua-Vitae, made and sold, to be paid by the Maker thereof'. The Act also made provision for 'Gagers ... at all times, as well by Night as by Day' and empowered them to enter 'the Distilling house'. The gagers (or gaugers, literally 'measurers') were officers recruited by landowners to evaluate and collect duty. In coastal districts they were supported by customs officers: 'tide-waiters' or 'tidesmen', who boarded ships to make sure they didn't land illicit cargo (brandy, tobacco and salt being the main items) en route to their port of destination. The responsibility for checking cargoes as they were being unloaded was mainly that of the 'land-waiters'. After about 1800, this was done by 'riding officers', who, armed with cutlasses and pistols, were empowered to pursue suspected contraband inland, including even searching the houses of the gentry. They received their orders from the 'surveyor' and the head of the customs staff in each district, known as

Exisemen with a confiscated still, c.1890.

the 'collector', who was directly responsible to Their Honours the Commissioners for customs and excise in Edinburgh.

The use of the term 'distilling house' in the Act of 1660 is interesting, as until 1689 there is no record of any commercial distilleries. However, many large households and castles had their own still-house, often combined with their brew-house; rural communities shared facilities and sometimes appointed one of their members (often a woman) as brewer/distiller.

The first commercial distillery we know about was the 'ancient brewary [sic] of aquavity' at Ferintosh on the Black Isle in Ross and Cromarty. In October 1689 it was burnt down by supporters of the exiled King James VII (II of England), as its owner, Duncan Forbes of Culloden, was an ardent Whig and a supporter of William of Orange. When the Jacobite Rising of 1688–89 had been suppressed, Forbes's son, also named Duncan, claimed compensation of £54,000 for the loss of the distillery. He received £21,540 but was also granted the privilege of distilling whisky duty-free from grains grown on his own lands upon payment of a trivial annual sum of 400 merks (around £22).

Within months of the passing of the 1660 Excise Act, smuggling operations of all kinds sprang up, with only a small percentage of the spirit produced entered for duty. This is not surprising, for several reasons.

First, distilling whisky, like brewing beer, was widely considered to be a 'right of man' (or, one might say, 'of woman' since much domestic brewing and distilling was done by females), an opinion shared by most landowners, who, like magistrates and judges, were supposed to enforce the law. It was also in

A Nation of Smugglers

Woodcut of a sixteenth-century distilling operation by Domenico Beccafumi, c.1530.

their interest that their tenants should have whisky to barter against the cash payment of rent. As a result, when smugglers were brought to court the fines were often risible. Popular sentiment was squarely behind the smuggler. Stephen Sillett, author of *Illicit Scotch*, writes: 'Virtually everyone joined in the smuggling activities. In most cases the middle and lower classes did the donkey work, whilst the already wealthy merchants and landed gentry pocketed the bulk of the proceeds.'

Second, the tax was impossible to enforce in the Highlands and extremely difficult to police in more populated districts, ports and towns throughout Scotland, owing to the scarcity of customs and excise officers. As Sillett concludes, 'Seizures of smuggled goods were few and far between, and were usually attributable to information leaked to revenue officers, as a sequel to arguments among the smugglers themselves.'

Third, and most significantly in the Highlands, was the crucial link between brewing/distilling and economic survival. The Highland economy was pastoral – based on cattle. During the long winter months the cattle survived on draff, the nutritious husks and spent grains remaining after making beer or whisky. So important was the draff that a community would typically allocate a third of its most fertile land to the cultivation of barley (known as 'drink crop') rather than oats ('food crop') and other vegetables – a fact that astonished visitors from the south. Hay was not grown in the Highlands, and barley yielded two 'crops': whisky and cattle fodder.

Fourth, after the 'Glorious Revolution' of 1688, which exiled King James VII and II, a substantial portion of the population doubted the legitimacy of the new monarchs, William and Mary (Mary was James's niece, and William III and II his nephew; their succeeding him was problematic insofar as James had a legitimate son of his own), or at least used this as an excuse to flout an unpopular law. As Duncan Fraser writes in *The Smugglers*: 'To the Jacobites [smuggling] was not only profitable, it was a crusade against all that was anti-Jacobite, including the Government in London. And the very best people were involved in it, even the richest merchants and the landed gentry.'[3]

William and Mary, scourge of the Jacobites.

Making Whisky

Dennis McBain

The three ingredients required to make Scotch whisky are malted barley, spring water and yeast.

The procedure for producing malted barley involves steeping barley in spring water in a steep vessel for around 40 hours, during which the water is drained off and replaced with fresh water three times. As a result, the barley will swell, thereby preparing it for the next stage, when it will germinate and begin to grow. After the last water has been drained off, the barley is removed from the vessel and laid out on the floor to a depth of approximately 200 millimetres. Over the next four to five days the barley will generate heat and begin to produce small shoots. Throughout this growing period the barley must be turned over to prevent it overheating and the shoots clumping together. It is also necessary to ensure there is sufficient air to keep it fresh.

At this point the growing shoots produce enzymes, which are required to turn starch into sugar during mashing. The growing process is stopped when the required growth has been achieved. The malted barley is then put in a kiln to stop it growing, dry it and prepare it for milling.

During the milling stage, the malted barley is ground in a mill to create a flour called grist, to enable the sugars to be easily removed at the next stage, which is mashing. This involves mixing the grist with hot water in a vessel called a mash tun where the enzymes produced during the malting stage break down the starch into sugars. The resulting brown liquid, called wort, is then ready for fermentation.

The wort is poured into the fermentation vessel and is cooled to the required temperature before yeast is added. The conversion of the sugars to alcohol now begins. After three to four days, fermentation will end and the liquid, now called wash, will be around 9% alcohol and ready for distillation.

The distillation process is in two stages and is achieved using a wash still and a spirit still. In the first stage, the wash is heated in the wash still until the alcohol has been boiled off and the vapours condensed back to liquid by means of a cooling worm, or condenser. This clear liquid, referred to as low wines, is around 24% alcohol and will have to

A mash tun in operation.

Whisky casks ageing at Glenfiddich Distillery.

be boiled again in order to increase the alcohol strength to a level that is high enough to be used. This is done at the second stage of distillation by putting the low wines in the spirit still and boiling off the alcohol vapours – thereby increasing the strength to around 72% alcohol. At this point the amount of clear spirit to be taken off and put in an oak cask for maturation is determined. During maturation, the clear spirit changes colour and gains more flavour – depending on the type of cask used and the length of time spent maturing.

Those involved in illicit distilling would have used one still for carrying out both stages of distillation. To lessen the risk of being caught, the still was in two parts. The bottom, a large pot, most likely made of copper, could also have been used for domestic purposes, such as cooking and washing clothes. The top part, also of copper, would have been attached to the bottom and sealed with clay or a similar material, thereby enabling it to be quickly disassembled and hidden, if the warning was raised that excise officers, who would have easily recognised it as being part of a still, were approaching. The large pot that formed the bottom of the still would also have been used for steeping, mashing and fermenting the barley.

A story often told by older residents of the Cabrach concerns a fellow who had had too much to drink and on hearing of an approaching exciseman, in a panic, hastily buried the top of his still. Unfortunately, when sober, he could not remember where it was buried. If true, somewhere in the Cabrach the copper head of an illicit still is waiting to be discovered.

Juniper, which grew widely in the Cabrach, was an ideal fuel for firing an illicit still, as when burning it produces no smoke, the sight of which could have attracted unwanted attention. Juniper would also have been useful for cleaning the still before it was used. This is a practice which is carried out to this day, by distillers Wm Grant & Sons, before a new still is used for whisky production. The process involves boiling water in the stills, adding some juniper branches and then letting the juniper vapours travel through the system. This practice is called sweetening the still.

II
Union and Disorder

*'What the heart of Scotland had resisted for four hundred years
was at last accepted by its stomach'*

The Lion in the North, John Prebble

To the dismay of many, but out of necessity, the 1707 Act of Union brought together the parliaments of England and Scotland. The disastrous attempt to become a trading nation by establishing a colony at Darien in South America had swallowed up 50 per cent of all the money circulating in Scotland, thereby creating a public debt of £400,000, which would be liquidated by the Union.

Despite having large Lowland areas of fertile arable land, and even wider tracts of pasture for cattle and sheep, Scotland was one of the poorest and most backward countries in Europe. Agriculture and animal husbandry, as well as mining and fisheries, were at the same stage as centuries before and would remain so for the first half of the eighteenth century.

Agriculture was entirely communal and generally provided only the barest subsistence. The margin between survival and starvation was narrow. This was further compounded by years of poor harvest, cattle disease and more than four successive seasons (1695–99), known among Jacobites as 'King William's ill years', during which the summers were so wet that crops failed and the peats cut in the spring were still sodden by the time winter arrived. Between a fifth and a third of the population died from starvation.[4] It was during these years of famine that molasses came into greater use for spirit distillation in Britain.

A subsistence economy implies payment in kind. As such, there is little doubt that whisky was used in part-payment of rent since cash was scarce and could not be won unless produce and goods could be taken to market. Even in the Lowlands few roads could cope with wheeled vehicles, which made it extremely difficult, if not impossible, for communities to sell their produce at any distance. If the roads in the Lowlands were bad, those in the Highlands were almost non-existent before the 1720s: mere tracks with numerous river crossings that could only be made at fords or by oar-powered ferries, low ground which was liable to flooding, and hill passes that were often choked with snow. Throughout the region, however, there was an intricate network of drove roads running east and south into the Lowlands along which cattle could be taken to market.

Droving increased throughout the seventeenth and eighteenth centuries, and by the 1780s, 150,000 head of cattle, sheep and horses from the Highlands

were changing hands at the great trysts of Falkirk alone. With them came whisky, in small oval casks called 'ankers', lashed to the sides of shaggy black cattle.

Immediately following the Act of Union, a Scottish Excise Board manned by English officials was established in Edinburgh and duty was levied at the same rate as in England (1d per gallon on spirits made for sale). There were mutterings of discontent – all things English were viewed with suspicion, especially those emanating from Westminster – which became a clamour when, in 1713, Parliament proposed to extend the Malt Tax from England to Scotland. Although this was to be at half the English rate, it would still double the tax payable in Scotland. When Queen Anne was succeeded by 'German Geordie', Elector of Hanover, as King George I, it was estimated that three-quarters of the country was now against the Union.

'Bobbing John', Earl of Mar, raised King James VIII and III's standard on 6 September 1715, calling upon all good men to fight for their rightful king, for

The Battle of Sheriffmuir, 1715.

the 'relief of our native country from oppression and a foreign yoke too heavy for us and our posterity to bear'. Many Highland chiefs brought out their clans; Perth was occupied, and Preston (briefly), but the Duke of Argyll held the Stirling Plain for the government with 5,000 men. On 13 November, they confronted the Jacobite army at Sheriffmuir in the Ochil Hills near Dunblane. The result of the battle was inconclusive, as a current ballad put it:

> A battle there was that I saw, man.
> And we ran, and they ran,
> And they ran, and we ran,
> And we ran, and they ran awa', man.

By December, when King James, 'the Old Pretender', arrived at Peterhead from France, the rising was over.

III
Ancient Liberties

'Had you seen these roads before they were made,
You would lift up your hands and bless General Wade'

Inscription on Wade's bridge across the River Tay at Aberfeldy

Major-General George Wade was appointed Commander-in-Chief in Scotland and set about constructing roads and bridges in the Highlands to allow troops to be quickly deployed 'in defence of the realm'. Together with his successor, William Caulfield, they laid down 750 miles of road and 79 elegant bridges. These made both the cattle drovers' and the smugglers' task easier – not surprisingly, there was a steady increase in the quantity of illicit whisky carried into the Lowlands.

The Malt Tax was finally implemented in 1725 to be greeted by a brewers' strike in Edinburgh and serious rioting in Glasgow, during which 11 people died. The city's Member of Parliament, Daniel Campbell of Shawfield, who had voted for the tax, had his house looted. In compensation, he was awarded £9,000, with which he bought the island of Islay.

In general, whisky consumption was stimulated by the Malt Tax, while ale drinking decreased. Previously, 'tuppeny ale' had been by far the most popular drink amongst the masses. This is witnessed by the fact that in 1708 only 50,800 gallons (228,600 litres) of whisky were sold under licence, compared with 288,000 barrels of ale – the price of the latter rose, and its quality declined.[5] It is therefore perhaps not surprising that many turned to whisky. The quantity

General George Wade's magnificent bridge across the River Tay at Aberfeldy

Ancient Liberties

The arrival of smugglers selling their goods: a sketch by Sir David Wilkie, c.1824.

of spirit distilled under licence doubled during the year 1724–25 to just over 100,000 gallons (450,000 litres) – excluding the duty-free output of Ferintosh – all produced in the Lowlands and made possible by using mixed grains, as well as malted barley. Highland whisky became even more popular, and cheaper, than that made in the Lowlands, as it evaded the tax. It goes without saying that the quantity of illicit whisky sold that year is unknown.

The middle and upper classes preferred imported gin and brandy – most of it smuggled – and of course claret, which for centuries had been the drink of choice for many Scots, along with home-brewed ale, which was drunk at breakfast (before tea became popular and widely available towards the middle of the eighteenth century). The domestic accounts of country houses often list large quantities of claret: 'Bumper John' Forbes of Culloden (whose younger brother, Duncan, was appointed Lord Advocate in 1725, and Lord Justice General, Scotland's highest legal appointment, in 1737) always had a cask placed in the corner of the hall, from which the contents were doled out by the pailful; as late as 1750, the accounts at Arniston House in East Lothian show the annual consumption of claret to be 16 hogsheads (840 gallons, or slightly over 3,800 litres).[6]

The account books from Broomhall Estate, near Dunfermline, list a staggering 7,638 gallons of mainly malt whisky being supplied to Lord Elgin's provisions merchant in the village of Charlestown on the estate between February 1824 and February 1827. The whisky came from Eastbridge Distillery (Kirkcaldy), Grange Distillery (Burntisland), Cowie Distillery (St Ninian's,

Stirling) and Canonmills Distillery (Edinburgh), was all at 100 or 90 proof, and was consumed by the inhabitants of only 138 cottages.[7]

Brandy, rum, gin, wine, tea – all these beverages were smuggled. As Gavin Smith remarks, smugglers 'would choose whichever commodities yielded the greatest profit at the time, switching merchandise as duty on various items rose and fell . . . Tea could be bought for 7d a pound on the Continent, and sold in Britain for 2/6d. Brandy and gin profit margins were even more attractive – a £1 cask could sell for £4, and if cut to drinking strength before sale, the margins were significantly higher.'[8] The profit on a cask of foreign spirits could be 400 to 500 per cent, and it was said that if one cargo in three was landed without detection, a profit would be made.

In *The Heart of Midlothian*, Sir Walter Scott writes, 'smuggling was almost universal during the reigns of George I and II; for the people, unaccustomed to imposts, and regarding them as an unjust aggression upon their ancient liberties, made no scruple to elude them wherever it was possible to do so'.

Indeed, even before the imposition of the Malt Tax, smuggling seems to have increased and become more violent. The customs service was hopelessly understaffed: for example, there were never more than 15 men to cover the 25-mile-long 'smuggler's coast' of Angus. By 1723, the tidesmen (the foot-soldiers of the service) at Arbroath were afraid to reveal the names of known smugglers. The following year, the Collector of Customs reported to his masters that 'if our officers happen to see any running goods, they are immediately mobbed, and the goods carried off by persons in women's habits. Neither is any of them to be prevailed with to discover who these persons are, they are so attached to one another'; and even if they made an arrest, 'there being no Law nor justice to be expected, the magistrates being tradesmen and affray'd to disoblige the merchants'.[9]

A *Parliamentary Inquiry into Frauds Upon the Revenue*, under the chairmanship of Sir John Cope, reported in 1736, 'The smugglers being grown to such a degree of insolence, as to carry on their wicked practices by force and violence, not only in the country and the remote parts of the Kingdom, but even in the City of London itself, going in gangs armed with swords, pistols and other weapons.'[10]

It is obvious the authorities were in an impossible position: if even the 'magistrates and merchants' turned a blind eye to smuggling, one can imagine what the attitude of the general populace was.

This was dramatically demonstrated by the Porteous Riot in Edinburgh, vividly described by Sir Walter Scott, which occurred in the same year as Sir John Cope's report. A mob lynched the captain of the City Guard, John Porteous, who had ordered the soldiers under his command to fire into the crowd during the execution of a popular smuggler from Pittenweem in Fife.

Ancient Liberties

When news of the fracas reached London, the authorities feared that it was part of an organised insurrection, probably Jacobite.

Captain Edward Burt, an English officer who accompanied General Wade into Scotland, provides a vivid and sympathetic picture of life in Scotland during the 1730s: 'The glory of the country is Usky,' he writes, '... the ruddy complexion and nimbleness of these people is not owing to the water drinking, but to Aqua Vitae, a malt spirit which is commonly used as both a victual and a drink.'[11]

He also remarks: 'Some of the Highland Gentlemen are immoderate drinkers of Usky, even three or four Quarts at a Sitting; and in general the People that can pay the Purchase, drink it without Moderation ... I have been tempted to think that this Spirit has in it, by Infusion, the Seeds of Anger, Revenge and Murder (this I confess is a little too poetical) but those who drink of it to any Degree of Excess behave for the most Part, like true Barbarians, I think much beyond the Effect of other Liquors.'[12]

The Porteous Mob wreaking havoc, Edinburgh, 1736, by James Drummond.

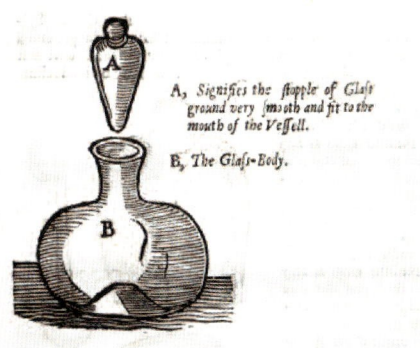

Illustration of a glass bottle and its lid from the *Art of Distillation*, 1651.

The Jacobite Legacy

Murray Pittock

Among the many changes brought by the Acts of Union were changes governing taxation. These were controversial long before they were agreed or came into effect. Tracts such as *The rights and interests of the two British monarchies* (1703) asked 'How are the People likely to be pleased with their Incorporating Union, when they must pay six pence for a Scots Pint of Ale, which they us'd to buy for Twopence'. When Union eventually took effect on 1 May 1707, there was widespread concern at the apparently unseemly haste with which English tax officers appeared in Scotland. Many of the Edinburgh brewers stopped brewing. Within a year, excise officers were everywhere at risk of attack for carrying out their duties, as the protectionism of the domestic market in beer in particular gave way to a most unwelcome combination of free trade and taxation.

The issue continued to be key in the development of the Malt Tax Bill of 1713, which was seen as a violation of the Union and led to a campaign for its repeal, headed by the Duke of Argyll and his brother, the Earl of Ilay, which only narrowly failed. Given the toxic and explosive political nature of the tax, the British government did not pursue it wholeheartedly in Scotland, but in 1724 Robert Walpole – more secure after the defeat of Jacobite designs in the 1722–23 Atterbury Plot – ensured that the Malt Tax would be collected in Scotland, and at a heavy rate. The tax was seen as a differential one in England's favour. Both beer and such whisky production as there was, were now under threat and there were riots in many Scottish burghs, most seriously in Glasgow in 1725, where troops were used to quell disorder. Indeed, the coming of the Malt Tax may also have accelerated the residence of General Wade in Scotland and his Highland road-building programme. In 1729, Walpole further increased duty on cheap spirits.

Throughout the first half of the eighteenth century, smugglers in both England and Scotland

left.
James III, the Old Pretender, by Alexis Belle.

Opposite.
Charles Edward Stuart, the young Bonnie Prince Charlie, by William Robertson, c.1735.

distributed high-cultural propaganda such as medals, prints and portraits. Coastal ports were a prime location for Jacobite spies and smugglers, and therefore made good clearing houses for Jacobite information. Sympathetic landlords aided smugglers for political and economic reasons. The four Smuggling Acts passed in England in 1698, 1717, 1721 and 1745 were introduced amid concern for Jacobite activity: each one occurred within two years or less of a major plot or rising. By 1745, a year after the major French invasion scare that was a prelude to the 'Forty-five' rising, the death penalty was prescribed for assembling to run goods or harbouring smugglers, with collective fines on whole counties for unsolved offences.

In Scotland an increase in smuggling was the response – not least on the east coast – to shrinking markets and discriminatory taxation, which reinforced the often Jacobite politics of those who pursued it. A successful Stuart restoration was seen as possibly limiting, if not cancelling, the national debt, thus lowering the indirect taxes needed to pay British government stockholders. This would lessen the upwards revenue pressure on excise and related duties. Thus a Stuart restoration would create a win-win environment for smugglers, where working towards a restoration now would allow them to evade tax, and a successful outcome to their efforts would lead to its diminution or abolition. Smuggling as a consequence – Jacobite smuggling – was often big business: its politicised nature as a crime and its degree of acceptance within the community surely played a significant role in the fury that led to the Porteous Riots in 1736. The fact that John Porteous had ordered his men to fire into the crowd at the execution of one of the three convicted smugglers, leading to six deaths, enraged the city of Edinburgh because of not only the deaths but also the original crime – smuggling – which was seen by quite a number of people as a patriotic act.

While initially there had been comparatively few Scots in exile with the Jacobite court and its supporters, after the defeat of the 1715 Rising their numbers increased markedly. It remained easy for Scots to naturalise in France, and they formed links with fellow anglophone supporters of the Stuarts, notably the Irish merchants who often settled on the coast, trading in brandy and wine. Traffic in these commodities between Scotland and France became a natural screen for Jacobite correspondence, and the Jacobitism of Leith no doubt had a connection to its role as a leading port for Continental trade. Smuggling was a crime associated with Jacobite activity in any case, and the imposition of the Malt Tax further politicised the production and traffic in more native forms of alcohol. In this politically toxic combination, the British government was seen as destroying the domestic drinks industry, while imported wines and spirits combined evading duty with bringing promises of support and a prospective end to Union by force of arms to the inhabitants of the east coast ports. Jacobite administrations during the Rising of 1715 (and indeed 1745) made a great play of returning to pre-Union taxation arrangements. It was no wonder in such a context that smuggling came to be seen as a patriotic option: a statement of the defence of the national interest of Scotland and its ancient line of kings against the oppressive abuse of the Union by a London Whig government. If even Scottish Whigs like Argyll could think of breaking the Union over this issue, what must have been the outlook of an Episcopalian from Montrose or Aberdeen, existentially opposed to the British state and not just its abuse of its legitimate power? In 1745, Montrose supplied significant numbers of Jacobites to the army of the prince, Charles Edward (the Young Pretender, Bonnie Prince Charlie), proportionately far more than would be expected from a town of its size.

While smuggling in England in the Jacobite era needs to be seen as often linked to political resistance as well as tax evasion, in Scotland in the same period it had a national quality: it was the patriotic option, a resistance to English taxes seen as discriminatory, punitive and anti-Scottish. The contraband patriotism of the Scottish drinks industry in the eighteenth century played an important part in the creation of a national drink.

IV
Open Transgression

'Come, let me know what it is that makes a Scotchman happy'

Dr Samuel Johnson, calling for a gill of whisky, quoted by James Boswell in
The Journal of a Tour to the Hebrides.

In 1755, Dr Samuel Johnson published his *Dictionary of the English Language*, confusingly defining 'usquebaugh' (i.e. *uisge beatha*) as 'a compounded distilled spirit, being drawn on aromaticks; and the Irish sort is particularly distinguished for its pleasant and mild flavour. The Highland sort is somewhat hotter; and, by corruption, the Scottish call it *whisky.*'

The amount of whisky that can be made – privately or commercially, legally or illegally – depends upon the quantity of grain available to be distilled. The year after Johnson's *Dictionary* was published the harvests were so bad that in March 1757 the government banned all distilling in Great Britain, renewing this imperative annually until December 1760. Many licensed distilleries closed, reducing the output of licensed spirits to one-ninth of what it had been in 1756, in which year tax was paid on 433,811 gallons of spirits.

A match made in heaven: James Boswell and Samuel Johnson, who commented on Scotch whisky in his dictionary.

Sampling the goods, Sir Edwin Landseer.

Private distilling was unaffected, 'so long as the spirits were not offered for sale'. It is perhaps not surprising that there was a dramatic increase in the quantity of illicit spirits put on the market. John Scott, an excise officer in Edinburgh, estimated that in the 1760s private distillers were producing around 500,000 gallons a year – about ten times the amount of legal production. 'Since 1757,' Scott wrote, 'smuggling has supplied the increased market. A number of poor people known by the name of private distillers have since that time simply supplied the demand for aqua vitae to the very great prejudice of the revenue [and] the public distillers.'[13]

Forbes of Culloden, whose family had been granted the licence to distil duty-free at Ferintosh in 1689, was also unaffected by the dire problems faced by the other licensed distilleries. Like many of his contemporaries, he was an enthusiast for the novel farming methods which were being adopted throughout Scotland, particularly in the Lowlands, during the so-called Agricultural Revolution, which greatly increased yields of corn and vegetables. He enlarged Ferintosh in the 1760s and built a further three distilleries on his estate, acquiring more land at Cromarty to grow barley. By the early 1770s he was producing 90,000 gallons annually – almost twice the amount of all the other licensed distilleries added together – and making a profit of £18,000 a year, more than £2 million today.[14]

His brother, Duncan Forbes, Lord Justice General and Lord President of the Court of Session, noted in *Some Considerations on the Present State of Scotland* (1744) that smuggling was causing significant damage to the economy and the Exchequer:

Wide and ill-guarded as the coasts of *Scotland* are [his italics throughout], the *Running* Trade could never have succeeded without the Assistance of the Inhabitants of the Sea-Coast. The *Smuggler* must have *Boats* to lay his goods on land; he must have *Cover* to shelter them in, until *Carriages* are provided; he must be possessed to the favourable Disposition of the People, to secure against Informations to the Customhouse; nay, he must be confident of their *Power* to protect his goods from Seizure, or to *rescue* them, if by Accident they should be seized. All these Aids are *indispensibly* necessary, and yet all of these Aids the *Felon*, who has been *murdering* his country, has hitherto had. *Gentlemen* and *Farmers* go on in the usual Train, cherishing and hugging to their Bosom the *Smuggler*, that *Leech* that lives by sucking their Heart's Blood …

In England … the goods run are a *trifle*, compared with the *regular importation*. But, in Scotland, every body knows that the matter stands *quite* otherwise. The *Smuggling* Trade is much *overdone*. The Facility of Running has invited every petty Dealer to try it. No foreign spirits *are*, and no Tea can be regularly imported into this country.[15]

The expansion of smuggling and the growth of the output from Ferintosh forced the few remaining licensed distillers to resort to fraud in order to survive. Concerned about the decline in its income, the Revenue attempted to tighten

Below.
Waiting patiently: an illicit distiller and his still. Sketch by Diane Sutherland.

Overleaf.
In both Scotland and Ireland illicit distilling was often a family affair. Painting by Sir David Wilkie, 1840.

its supervision of commercial distilleries: in 1772 an Act was passed which required excise locks and seals on all vessels, particularly the heads of stills, so they could not be operated without the knowledge of the authorities. This was followed two years later by an Act prohibiting distillation in small stills (wash stills less than 400 gallons and spirit stills less than 100 gallons), which acted as a virtual prohibition of distilling in the Highlands, where smaller stills than this were general. Such measures merely discouraged distillers from 'entering' (i.e. taking out licences) and as a result stimulated smuggling.

By the 1770s, agricultural improvements were increasing the yield of cereal grains all over Lowland Scotland, the surpluses enabling distilling on a much larger scale than had been hitherto possible. As Moss and Hume attest in *The Making of Scotch Whisky*, the largest of these 'great and middle-class distilleries' were in Fife and Edinburgh, and represented 'the largest manufacturing undertakings of any kind to emerge during the first decade of the industrial revolution in Scotland'.[16] Almost all were owned by generations of the Stein and Haig families, who virtually controlled legal distilling in Central Scotland during the later decades of the century.

Demand for whisky was steadily increasing, not only from the growing urban population, swelled by former cottars and farm tenants who could no longer find work in the rural areas, but also amongst the middle and upper classes, for whom it was now fashionable to drink it as punch. Between 1777 and 1779 the consumption of legally made whisky trebled, and it may be safely estimated that the consumption of 'pure and wholesome' illicit whisky increased even more.

In his *History of Edinburgh*, Hugo Arnot estimated that in 1777 there were 400 illicit stills operating in the city, while there were only eight entered distilleries. Arnot also noted that of the 2,011 taverns in Edinburgh at the time only 159 were licensed to sell foreign spirits; the remaining 1,852 were 'for the entertainment of the lower classes of person', and sold only ale and whisky, much of it illicit.

Furthermore, as David Bremner writes:

About the year 1776 a demand for Scotch spirits sprang up in England, and large quantities were sent thither. An import duty of 2/6d [12.5p] a gallon was charged in England; and an extensive system of smuggling also sprang up. It is stated that in 1787 upwards of 300,000 gallons crossed the Border without the knowledge of the Excise.[17]

In the Borders, illicit stills were thought to have outnumbered legal operations fiftyfold.

Ross Wilson in *Scotch Whisky Made Easy* notes:

> Known production of Scotch whisky began to be recorded in 1708. In that year about 50,000 gallons were listed. Within fifty years it had risen to over 400,000 gallons. Within a further twenty years [i.e. c.1778] . . . something like 300,000 gallons were reliably estimated as being *smuggled* [his italics] across the border into England – apart from a similar amount which was entering England legally.

To combat the illicit trade, the 'great and middle class distillers' formed a monopoly and flooded the market with cheap spirits. In this they were supported by the landowners, who were also nervous about the rise in foreign imports, particularly French brandy. Both felt their interests to be severely compromised by the flood of illicit goods. From the government's point of view, if distilling were concentrated within the larger Lowland concerns, the collection of duties would be much easier. Accordingly, in 1778, import duties were increased by eight guineas a butt on French wine and brandy (four guineas on other foreign wines and spirits). But, as invariably happens, the increase in duty led to an increase in smuggling. It also encouraged the not-so-well-off to turn to whisky.

In March 1783, one George Bishop of Maidstone, Kent, submitted a pamphlet for consideration by HM Government, arguing that duties should be reduced in order to make smuggling less attractive:

> Both in England and in Scotland smuggling is now carried on to a considerable extent, greatly promoted by the high duties on British spirits; in London and Bristol are many private distillers who make large quantities of spirits without paying duties, and in Scotland there are upwards of ten thousand private stills which make and send immense quantities of spirits to London with some others that have paid the duties, to the very great hurt of the honest trader, by which practise the revenue has been defrauded of upwards of £100,000 this year . . .
>
> In the year 1777 there was smuggled from Dunkirk 2,500,000 gallons of Geneva [jenever, known as Dutch gin], about which time there were established at Gottenburg, Newport, Ostend, Dunkirk and Calais distilleries for making Geneva to supply our smugglers with.[18]

Kent, where Mr Bishop resided, was among the leading smuggling counties in England, but the illicit trade was far more prevalent in Scotland than south of the Border:

> Smuggling was carried on far more largely in Scotland than in England, for the Scots fair-traders [as the smugglers termed themselves] were

A plan of the town of Dunkirk, 1706. By 1777, over two million gallons of jenever were being smuggled from the port.

satisfied with smaller profits, and it was executed with more security, as the people helped and encouraged them in resisting customs that were imposed by the English. A vast deal of harm was done by this illicit trade to the inhabitants of the sea-coast – it encouraged a spirit of gambling in their life, it demoralised their tone, it discouraged all active, steady pursuit among those who might have lived by honest fishing in the sea or working on the land. But still the trade went on.[19]

In 1779, An Act for the Prevention of Frauds by Private Distillers reduced the permitted size of still for domestic distilling from ten to two gallons, making it impossible to produce spirits surplus to household requirements. Then, in 1781, private distilling for domestic consumption was banned altogether. Excise officials were instructed to seize stills and spirits, destroy wash and utensils, and, if required, draw on help from the military. From now on, and for the first time ever, all home distilling became 'illicit' and the main concern of the revenue authorities turned from the illegal importation of foreign spirits to the local production and transportation of whisky. The following year, no less than 1,940 illicit stills were seized, over half of them in the Highlands.

The Act was widely thought to be 'injudicious, vexatious and injurious';[20] a

Open Transgression

Smugglers: 'To save their necks' (1889–1903), by Charles Napier Hemy.

direct intervention in an immemorial personal right. Scottish farmers had always made whisky, just as farmers in Somerset had always made cider. Distilling was an essential part of the eternal cycle of the farming year, using up surplus grains, supplying farmers with nutritious winter feed for their cattle and providing communities with 'wholesome cheer' in the winter months. The Highlanders felt particularly discriminated against. Moreover, because of the 1774 Act banning the use of small stills, legal distilling in the Highlands was virtually prohibited. Anyone who wanted to distil was obliged to work outside the law.

This time there was no popular outcry; no riots like those condemning Captain Porteous or the Malt Tax earlier in the century. In truth, so many private distillers had been running illicit operations for so long that it was very much 'business as usual'. Indeed, business improved: 'The smuggler's gain was in direct proportion to the amount of spirit duty; the higher the duty the greater the gain and the stronger the temptation'.[21] To encourage the detection and seizure of illicit stills, a premium of 1s 6d was payable to informants and excise officers. The smugglers cheerfully informed the gaugers of the whereabouts of their old equipment, undoubtedly with the latter's connivance, and put the bounty they received towards a new still. In spite of the seizure of nearly 2,000

stills in 1782, it was estimated that there were 21,000 stills in operation in the Highlands.[22]

These were years of dearth. Notwithstanding the improvements in farming, harvests failed in 1782, 1783 and 1784. Famine stalked the Highlands as it had done during King William's ill years nearly a century before. The Commissioners of Supply in several Highland counties banned distilling altogether and the government sought to limit the amount of grain going to the distillers by doubling duty to four shillings per gallon of spirit. As a result, the consumption of (legal) whisky dropped by almost 50 per cent in the year 1783.

Partly in response to the plight of the Highlands and partly to facilitate the collection of duty in the Lowlands, where the large commercial distilleries were located, the government introduced a measure which altered the basis upon which excise duty was founded. The Wash Act of 1784 drew a notional barrier diagonally across Scotland – the 'Highland Line' – with different rates of duty and other provisions above and below.

Geologically, the line follows the Highland Boundary Fault, which bisects the country from Helensburgh in the south-west to Stonehaven in the northeast, but historically this divide was as much linguistic and cultural as geological: to the north and west lay the wild Highlands and its equally savage Gaelic-speaking clans; to the south and east lay the douce Lowlands, anglophone and comparatively richer in agriculture and trade.

The Highland Line was originally drawn to include all areas within the counties (excluding Cromarty) north of the Firth of Tay and west of the Firth of Clyde. Also included were Lanarkshire, Dumbartonshire, Stirlingshire and Perthshire. The line was redrawn in 1785 and 1787, and the areas reduced.

Below the line (and in England) distillery duties were lowered considerably; instead of being imposed on low wines and spirits, it was now assessed on the wash from which the low wines were distilled. The original assessment was at 5d per gallon, on the assumption that five gallons of wash produced one gallon of spirit (at between 55% and 65% ABV). If more were produced, it would be forfeit. Earlier regulations concerning the minimum size of stills (400 gallons for wash stills; 100 gallons for spirit stills) and the stringent control of plant and operations remained in place. All movement of spirits had to be accompanied by an excise permit and distillers planning to export to England had to give notice.

Above the line the regulations were more liberal, partly to encourage smugglers to take out licences, partly in recognition of the recent famine, and also on account of the difficulty of assessing wash in small distilleries. Stills of 20 gallons were permitted (30 gallons in larger parishes), with duty payable at £1 per gallon per year. Only one still was permitted per distillery; only grain grown within the parish could be used and the spirit made had to be consumed

The 1784 Wash Act set different rates of duty for Highland and Lowland distillers. A notional barrier – the Highland Line – running from the south-west to the north-east, divided the country.

within the district. Infringements carried heavy penalties, which the heritors (landowners) of the parish had to pay if the distiller failed to. Ferintosh Distillery's 'perpetual right' to distil free of duty was revoked (with a payment of £21,580 compensation – estimated at about £2.2 million today – to Forbes of Culloden).

The measures satisfied nobody. Highland landowners were outraged at possibly having to pay fines, Lowland distillers were furious about what they saw as Highland privileges and the Board of Excise was doubtful about applying the provisions. Under pressure from the landed interest and Lowland distillers, the following year William Pitt's government passed an Amending Act, which forbade the movement of whisky made legally in the Highlands and beyond. It also limited the number of distillery licences to two per parish, restricted the amount of grain used and increased the permissible still size to 30 gallons (40 in larger parishes) – with duty assessed at the slightly increased rate of £1 10s [150p] per gallon capacity. As a sop to Highland landowners, the provision that heritors should pay fines was removed, substituting instead the proviso that distillers should be 'respectable tenants'.

In relation to Lowland distilling, it abolished the tax on wash and applied the Highland system of taxing still capacity, at the higher rate of £2 10s per gallon of capacity, which was based on declarations by the London distillers to a House of Commons Committee that stills could be discharged seven times a week if 'good quality spirit was to be made'.

The wily Lowland distillers ignored this caveat and designed shallow stills with broad, saucer-shaped bases that could be charged and distilled many times more than once. The resulting spirit was impure and unpleasant, fit only to be rectified and compounded into gin, which much of it was. Although some was made palatable by the addition of sugar and lemons, to make punch, drinkers increasingly sought out whisky made above the Highland Line and imported illegally into the Lowlands.

Components of a tin pot-still of the type commonly used by illicit distillers.

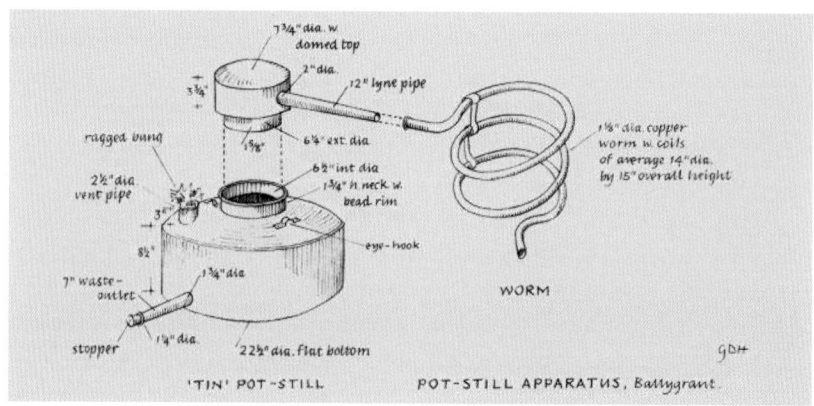

V
Distilling in a Thousand Hands

'Smuggling has grown to an alarming extent, and if it is not checked will undermine the best principles of the people . . .'

Colonel David Stewart of Garth, *Sketches of the Character, Manners and Present State of the Highlanders of Scotland*

In early 1793 war was declared with the nascent French Republic. Immediately, Lowland duty was tripled to £9 per gallon of still capacity; in the Highlands, it remained at £1 10s. Two years later this was hiked to £54 per gallon and Highland duties raised by £1. In 1797, the Highland tax was increased to £3 and an 'intermediary area' adjacent to the Highland Line was created in which licences were fixed at £9. This area remained for only two years, after which it became part of the Lowland region. The same Act (1800) again doubled Lowland duties to £108 per gallon of still capacity – a dramatic increase on the £3 it had been ten years before. By 1803, it was £162.

The war exacerbated the economic situation in the Highlands, where many

Tax revenue for the years 1791–1867.

Years	England. Duty per Gallon.	Scotland. Lowland.	Scotland. Highland.	Ireland. Duty per Gallon.	Paid Duty in Scotland for Consumption.
		Duty per Gallon of Still Contents.			
	£ s. d.	£ s. d.	£ s. d.	£ s. d.	Gallons.
1791	0 3 4¾	3 12 0	1 4 0	0 1 1¼	
1794	0 3 10¾	10 16 0½	1 16 0	0 1 1¼	
1797	0 4 10¼	64 16 4	3 0 0	0 1 5¼	
1800	0 5 4¼	64 16 4	7 16 0¼	0 2 4¼	1,277,596
		Per Gallon Spirits made.			
1802	0 5 4¼	0 3 10½	0 3 4¼	0 2 10¼	1,158,558
1804	0 8 0½	0 5 9¾	0 5 0½	0 4 1	1,189,757
1807	0 8 0½	0 5 8¾	0 4 11¼	0 4 1	2,653,478
1811	0 10 2¾	0 8 0¼	0 6 7½	0 2 6½	1,951,092
		£ s. d.			
1815	0 10 2¾	0 9 4½		0 6 1½	1,591,148
1817	0 10 2¾	0 6 2		0 5 7¼	1,906,950
1823	0 11 8¼	0 2 4¾		0 2 4¾	2,303,286
1825	0 11 8¼	0 2 4¾		0 2 4¾	5,981,549
1826	0 7 0	0 2 10		0 2 10	3,988,788
1830	0 7 6	0 3 4		0 3 4	6,007,631
1840	0 7 10	0 3 8		0 2 8	6,180,138
1852	0 7 10	0 3 8		0 2 8	7,172,015
1853	0 7 10	0 4 8		0 3 4	6,584,648
1854	0 7 10	0 6 0		0 4 0	6,553,239
1856	0 8 0	0 8 0		0 6 2	7,175,939
1860	0 10 0	0 10 0		0 10 0	4,729,705
1864	0 10 0	0 10 0		0 10 0	5,014,121
1867	0 10 0	0 10 0		0 10 0	4,983,009

Opposite.
Keeping a watchful eye:
Smugglers, The Alarm,
H.P. Parker.

traditional sources of income (crofting, cattle-droving, fishing) were badly affected. Smuggling became a necessity for survival. The Lowland distillers fared better. Although the dramatic increases in duty drove several out of business, the larger operators survived by developing techniques of rapid distillation. In 1793, a minister at Kirkcaldy, Fife, reported in the monumental 29-volume *Statistical Account of Scotland* that the larger Lowland concerns could work off a still 25 times in 24 hours.[23]

In 1797, the Scottish Excise Board reported that John Stein's Canonmills Distillery had three stills of 253 gallons' capacity which were worked off at the 'rate of forty-seven charges and discharges . . . in the space of twelve hours – an improvement on dispatch almost incredible'. The report estimated that the larger Lowland distillers could discharge their stills 90 times in 24 hours.[24] As a result, distilling capacity in the Lowlands increased five-fold between 1795 and 1797, but the amount of duty accruing to the Revenue less than doubled.

Although the Highland and Lowland distillers remained at daggers drawn, all licensed distillers felt threatened by the quantity of illicit whisky which was now being made, particularly in the Highlands and smuggled into the Lowlands.

As Stein submitted in his evidence to the 1798 Parliamentary Committee on Distilleries:

> The distillery is in a thousand hands. It is not confined to great towns or to regular manufacturers, but spreads itself over the whole face of the country, and in every island from the Orkneys to Jura. There are many who practice this art who are ignorant of every other, and there are distillers who boast that they make the best possible Whiskey, who cannot read or write and who carry on the manufacture in parts of the country where the use of the plough is unknown, and where the face of the Exciseman was never seen. Under such circumstances, it is impossible to take account of its operations; it is literally to search for revenue in the woods or on the mountains.[25]

The minister of Killearnan in Ross-shire was somewhat more compassionate: 'Distilling is almost the only method of converting our victual into cash for payment of rents and servants; and what may in fact be called our staple commodity.'[26]

A number of factors coincided to encourage the illicit trade. A shilling's worth of malt could be converted into four shillings' worth of spirit, and the bere barley grown in the Highlands was good for little else. The residues – draff and dreg (as pot ale was termed) – provided highly nutritious winter feed for cattle. The cattle themselves were annually driven in their thousands to the

Lowland markets, providing easy cover for smuggling casks of whisky. Stills could be knocked up by the local coppersmith – in Inverness, 'the sign of the still' became the mark of the master coppersmiths' shops – and a ten-gallon still could be had for £5. When legal distilling was banned after poor harvests, as it was in 1800–01, 1809–11 and 1812, the smugglers met the by-now-huge demand for whisky. It was not surprising that, as one traveller remarked, 'The distillation of whisky presents an irresistible temptation to the poorer classes.'[27]

It was clear to the government that something must be done to simplify the customs and excise laws, which were contained in no fewer than 27 volumes and were not available for public scrutiny. When William Pitt the Younger became Prime Minister in 1783, he proposed the intelligent solution of simply cutting duties, in line with George Bishop's recommendations. In 1787, 2,615 different resolutions were approved by the House of Commons, but they were only partially effective.

The Highlands were becoming impossible to police. For example, in 1787, there was only one excise officer to cover the whole of the area between Dunkeld and Aviemore – so there was a good chance of evading detection. When cases were brought to court, Justices of the Peace were often sympathetic to the smugglers' cause – after all, the magistrates were also landowners, and tenants made prosperous by the sale of illicit spirits could afford to pay higher rents. In some cases magistrates went so far as to pay the fines themselves, perhaps setting it against the smuggling tenant's rent arrears.

Even if convicted, illicit distillers were treated with greater consideration by their gaolers than other prisoners. The offence was not considered to be heinous, and a spell in prison was not considered to be a disgrace or even much of a punishment. Some prison officers allowed their smuggling charges to go home at weekends. One John Macdonald of Strathpeffer was sentenced to six weeks in Dingwall gaol. After a fortnight he made a pact with his warder: each evening at dusk his cell door was unlocked to allow him to slip away and tend his still; each daybreak he was back with a jar of whisky for the gaoler.

In short, the temptations to make and sell illicit whisky far outweighed any considerations of law-breaking; indeed, the reverse was generally the case. Successful smugglers were often local heroes: 'To the smuggler, no stigma was attached on account of his employment; on the contrary, it was considered rather an honourable occupation, as exhibiting an intrepidity and art that acquired for their possessor a distinction in the minds of his companions.'[28]

Lord Justice Clerk Granton opined from the bench in the Inverness Circuit Court in October 1807, 'Smuggling is too commonly considered a very venial crime. It is considered as cheating the King but in truth it is theft of a very aggravated kind and is attended with consequences much to be deplored.'[29]

Whole communities – men, women and children – were involved in the

Distilling in a Thousand Hands

adventure. If the gaugers attempted a seizure, the entire population would attack them with sticks and stones.

Sillett writes:

> In the Highlands, nearly every farmer had his own still, and the greatest ingenuity was shown, not only in carrying out the various brewing and distilling processes, but in warning one another of the approach of the itinerant Exciseman. When the farmers saw the gauger approaching on horseback, they made haste to raise the alarm by hoisting sheets or flags on the tops of peat stacks, so as to give everyone a chance to hide their precious whisky and utensils.[30]

A well-known story about raising the alarm was that of Ellen Cumming of Cardow farm, Knockando parish, Speyside, whose husband John was an illicit distiller until 1824, and whose grandson became chairman of John Walker & Sons a century later. There were no inns in this part of Speyside, so when the gaugers visited the district they stayed at Cardow. As soon as Ellen had got them comfortable for dinner, she hoisted a red flag over the steading to warn her neighbours that the excisemen were in the vicinity and to give them time to hide their equipment.

Cabrach sunset: the minister Thomas Guthrie recalled the bands of men on horseback who 'scoured the plains, rattled into villages and towns' and disposed of their whisky 'to agents everywhere'. By 1787, the desolate Cabrach was becoming increasingly hard to police.

Bridge over the River Gairn on the Old Military Road, Strathdon.

In the *Statistical Account of Scotland*, Sir John Sinclair commented that illicit distilling in the Highlands was commonly a community operation. This made sense. If there was a successful raid by the Excise, the cost of replacing the kit was shared and fines imposed by the court were divided between members of what could be described as a 'co-operative'. If necessary, distilling operations could be moved from place to place in the parish to make the gaugers' job more difficult. Tasks associated with whisky-making could be allocated to members of the group, so that no one individual was absent from their 'day-time job' long enough to attract notice.

George Smith, who was a smuggler before he founded the first licensed distillery in Glenlivet in 1824, told the *London Scotsman* newspaper about a raid in Glenlivet, in which the local gauger was supported by 'the crew of a revenue cutter':

> They travelled all night, got into the glen unmolested, and the gauger's eyes were rejoiced to see some forty or fifty stills reeking away finely. But he soon saw another sight he did not like so well. The smugglers had been advised of their coming, and having collected to the number of several hundreds, suddenly made their appearance, and defied the gauger's party to molest a single still. The gauger had an idea of fighting; but the notion was banished by the cutter's men, who protested that their cutlasses and pistols were of no service against the splendid long guns with which the smugglers were armed.[31]

A minister in Strathdon, near Glenlivet, wrote that in the upland part of his parish, in the hills between Donside and Speyside, smuggling was endemic. 'The inhabitants of Corgarff, the glens and not a few in the lower part of the parish [are all] professed smugglers . . . to be engaged in illicit distillation, and to defraud the excise, was neither looked on as a crime, nor considered as a disgrace.'[32]

When it came to transporting the goods, large-scale, well-organised smuggling operations had been noted as early as 1790, when an official report complained of hosts of smugglers operating below the Highland Line, 'travelling in bands of fifty, eighty, or a hundred and hundred and fifty horses remarkably stout and fleet [having] the audacity to go in this formidable manner in the open day upon the public high roads and through the streets of such towns and villages as they have occasion to pass'.[33]

As a boy, Thomas Guthrie, who became a minister at Brechin in Angus, remembered the bands of 'Highland smugglers' which came down from the 'wilds of Aberdeenshire' or 'the glens of the Grampians':

> They rode on Highland ponies, carrying on each side of their small, but brave and hardy steeds, a small cask or 'keg' as it was called, of illicit whisky . . . when night fell, every man to horse, descending the mountains only six miles from Brechin, scoured the plains, rattled into villages and towns, disposing of their whisky to agents they had everywhere; and now safe returned at their leisure, often in triumphal procession. I have seen a troop of thirty of them riding in Indian file, and in broad day, through the streets of Brechin, after they had succeeded in disposing of their whisky, and, as they rode leisurely along, beating time with their formidable cudgels on the empty barrels to the great amusement of the public and mortification of the excisemen.[34]

It is highly likely that the whisky everyone drank was in reality illicit. Indeed, it was often respectable members of the middle class who masterminded the illicit trade.

The story of Magnus ('Mansie') Eunson provides a good illustration of this, as well as of how legends grew up around smugglers. No less an authority than Alfred Barnard tells us that Eunson, a brewer in Kirkwall, Orkney, who had a still in the High Park of Rosebank above the town (it would later become Highland Park Distillery), was 'the most accomplished smuggler in Orkney' and 'a United Presbyterian church officer'. He also recounts how, on hearing that the excise officers were about to search the kirk, where he had a cache of casks under the pulpit, he 'had the kegs removed to his house, placed in the middle of an empty room, and covered with a clean white cloth. As the officers

Overleaf.
Sea-Coast Scene, Smugglers by George Morland.

approached after their unsuccessful search in the church, Eunson gathered all his people, including the maidservants, round the whisky, which, with its covering of white, under which a coffin lid had been placed, looked like a bier. Eunson knelt at the head with the Bible in his hand and the others with their psalm books. As the door opened they set up a wail for the dead, and Eunson made a sign to the officers that it was a death, and one of the attendants whispered "smallpox". Immediately the officer and his men made off as fast as they could . . .'[35]

Professor Michael Moss has researched beyond the legend and reveals in *100 Years of Quality: A History of Highland Distilleries* that, in reality, Eunson's history was more prosaic. There is no record of his having been a kirk elder; more likely he was a small-time hood, and front-man for the respectable merchants and small gentry who backed the illicit trade in Orkney. In kirk and court records we see him being arraigned for using foul language, fined for brewing illegally, arrested for smuggling (mysteriously the case never came to court), fined for fattening cattle on the minister's land without permission, and stealing a horse and riding it to death in a night.

As well as the organised bands of freebooters, there was the easier option of hiding contraband among the huge herds of cattle which were driven down annually from the Highlands for sale in the Lowlands, including at the previously mentioned Falkirk Trysts, which, from the early 1770s until the arrival of the railway in the 1840s, were the principal cattle markets in Scotland.

In his *The Industries of Scotland*, David Bremner elegantly summarised the growth of smuggling during the late eighteenth century:

> Eighty or ninety years ago the illicit manufacture of whisky was common throughout the Highlands. At first the 'sma' stills' were set to work to produce a supply of whisky for the use of the owners and their friends; but as the restrictions on licensed distillers were increased, the proprietors of the unlicensed stills were encouraged to extend their operations, and to enter into competition with the legal manufactures. Then began that system of smuggling which made a certain class of Highlander so notorious, and gave so much trouble to the Excise department. The wild glens of the north afforded secure retreats for the working of the stills; and many ingenious modes of conveying the produce to market were devised. The tendency was to demoralise the smugglers, and cast them back towards barbarism. They became reckless and daring to an extraordinary degree, and the stories of smuggling adventures record the performance of acts which, had they been rendered in a legitimate service, would have conferred undying honour on the actors. A man who could 'jink the gauger' was a hero of the little

circle in which he moved, and the people of the rural districts generally hailed with delight the performance of any deed which set the Excise laws at defiance. Even persons in authority winked at the breach of those laws. The great strongholds of the smugglers in the north were Glenlivet, Strathdon and the Glen of New Mill.[36]

In popular mythology, the smugglers always defeat the grim gaugers with cunning ploys, being portrayed as quick-witted, good-humoured and tough, while expressing the hardy independence of the Highlander which was already so much admired when those same men wore the king's uniform and shed their blood in the French wars. On the other hand, the gaugers are usually depicted as 'plodding dim-wits', to use Derek Cooper's phrase, 'arriving at the wrong place at the wrong time, subjects of public mortification and universal derision'.[37]

John Marsden, riding officer, 1870, Maryport.

The reality was very different. Unlike almost every other area of civil service – including commissions in the army – entry to this cadre of government servants was by merit alone. Not even the commissioners of excise, who ran the show, could manipulate appointments and any suggestion of canvassing automatically debarred a candidate – as Robert Burns discovered in the late 1780s, when he desperately tried to pull strings to obtain an appointment as an exciseman.

The annual wage was £50, augmented by half the value of seizures and fines imposed in the event of a conviction. One good capture, if conviction followed, could be worth a year's salary, but, as we have seen, obtaining a conviction was difficult, since magistrates either dismissed the case or imposed nominal fines. Out of their meagre stipend riding officers had to meet all their needs, including a horse, as well as rewarding spies and informers (without whom discoveries were unlikely) and paying posses of 'deputies' to assist in seizures.

One only has to read Robert Burns' accounts of working as a riding officer to realise what a hard job it was. He wrote to Mrs Dunlop in October 1789 that since early the previous month he had been riding 'five days a week, up to 40 miles a day, ere I return, besides four different kinds of book-keeping', and to John Mitchell, 'I have broke my horse's wind, & almost broke my own neck, besides some injuries in a part that shall be nameless, owing to a hard-hearted stone of a saddle'.[38]

Some supervisors of excise augmented their income with bribes, sometimes assisted by their wives, who would inform smugglers' wives of intended searches

Pistols used by Robert Burns during his time as an excise officer.

in return for whisky and vegetables. In effect, the interests of officers and the men on the ground were at variance.

A compromise was struck by which riding officers, after making a seizure and collecting their share of the proceeds, would allow smugglers every opportunity to make good their losses before apprehending them a second time. As Sillett dryly puts it in *Illicit Scotch*: 'In this way both could reckon on showing a small profit at the end of the day.'

The work was always dangerous, and injury and even death became increasingly common after the start of the nineteenth century. Sir Osgood Mackenzie of Inverewe quotes his uncle, a Justice of the Peace: 'Why does any accident happening to a gauger give general pleasure – far more so than an accident to a policeman? I have heard of a Strathglass gauger being quietly murdered. It was known he would on such a day and hour be riding to where he knew a bothy was in full work. One part of the road wound round a corner where a step missed would probably land horse and rider one hundred feet below in a horrid rocky ravine. As he came round the corner a woman rose up from the side of the road and suddenly threw her gown over her head in an apparently innocent fashion to shelter herself from the wind; the horse instantly lurched over into the ravine, and both it and its rider soon died from the accident (?) to the sorrow (?) of the smugglers [Mackenzie's question marks].'[39]

Once a still, cache of whisky or a contraband-carrying convoy was discovered, neither smugglers nor gaugers gave any quarter. Pitched battles were sometimes fought, such as that which passed into song as 'The Battle of Corriemuckloch', waged in the hills between Crieff and Amulree in Perthshire and involving a detachment of Scots Greys.

Nobody loved a gauger: even Robert Burns described himself as 'a paltry exciseman' and considered his job to be an 'insignificant existence in the meanest of pursuits, among the vilest of mankind'.

The career of Malcolm Gillespie is a prime example of what might befall even the most ambitious of excise officers. He joined the excise service in 1799 and served as an exciseman for nearly 30 years, mainly at Collieston and Stonehaven on the east coast, then inland to the 'Skene Ride', between the Rivers Don and Dee, a notorious smuggling district. When he moved to the latter in 1816, he bought a 'bulldog' or mastiff, trained to seize the smugglers' horses by the nose, forcing them to rear up and throw off the casks they were carrying.

During his career, Gillespie 'seized or destroyed' 14,000 gallons of foreign spirits, 6,535 gallons of whisky, 407 stills, 165 horses, 85 carts and no less than 60,000 gallons of wash, but in spite of the 'seizure bonus' system, his expenses – which included paying for information and for three or four assistants (and their board and lodging) – were more than his income.[40]

In desperation he resorted to forging a couple of Treasury bills. He was discovered and tried in September 1827 at the High Court in Aberdeen, where he was found guilty and sentenced to death. On the scaffold, he was able to point to 42 wounds on various parts of his body received in government service. But he was hanged, nevertheless.

It has been said that the smugglers' gain was in direct proportion to the level of duty imposed upon spirits: as duties were increased to raise money for the Napoleonic Wars during the first decade of the nineteenth century, smuggling became better organised and more 'professional'. Its corrosive effect upon the morals of whole communities began to be noted, and now not only by the ministers of the Church, who had remarked in the *Statistical Account* about the moral degradation of their parishioners as smuggling became more widespread and better organised:

> Quite the most disturbing aspect of the high incidence of illicit distilling and smuggling in the Highlands in the early years of the nineteenth century was the way it served to undermine the morals and honesty of a hitherto mild and inoffensive people. A demoralising wave of drunkenness, debauchery, theft and dissoluteness engulfed the population, informers were brutally beaten up, and even murdered, and Sheriff's Officers went in terror of their lives whenever they were required to serve summonses upon smugglers.[41]

To compound the issue, distilling from grain was banned in 1801–02, 1809–11 and 1812, while dramming was now part of life for all levels of society. In his *Autobiography*, quoted above, Thomas Guthrie remarks: 'Everybody, with a few exceptions, drank what was in reality illicit whisky – far superior to that made under the eye of the Excise – lords and lairds, members of Parliament and ministers of the Gospel, and everybody else.'

Looking back to about 1812, Elizabeth Grant of Rothiemurchus recalls in her *Memoirs of a Highland Lady* that 'whisky was a bad habit . . . there was certainly too much of it going':

> At every house it was offered, at every house it must be tasted or offence would be given, so we were taught to believe . . . In our house . . . a bottle of whisky was the allowance per day, with bread and cheese in any required quantity, provided for anyone who visited Rothiemurchus House on Speyside.
>
> The very poorest cottage could offer whisky; all the men engaged in the wood manufacture drank it in goblets three times a day . . . a lad with a small cask – a quarter anker – on his back and a horn cup in his hand that held a gill [one-third of a pint] appeared three times a day

amongst them. They all took their 'morning' raw, undiluted and without accompaniment, so they did the gill at parting when the day was done; but the noontide dram was part of a meal.

Illicit distilling was by no means confined to remote rural districts. In July 1815, a 'private' distillery of considerable extent, which had been in operation for 18 months, was discovered under an arch of Edinburgh's South Bridge.

The bridge consists of a large number of arches [19 in all], only one of which is open, the others being blocked up by the houses which line the bridge on both sides. It was in one of these arches adjoining the open one that the distillery had been set up. All the arrangements for conducting the business without the knowledge of the Excise officers were of the most complete kind. The only entrance to the place was by a doorway situated behind the grate of a bedroom in a house on one of the lower flats adjoining the bridge. Between this doorway and the distillery, communication was established by means of a ladder and trap-door. A supply of water was obtained from a branch attached to

South Bridge, Edinburgh.

one of the mains of the Water Company which passed overhead, and the smoke and waste was got rid of by making an opening in the chimney of one of the adjoining houses, and establishing a communication with the soil pipes. The spirits were sent out in a tin case capable of containing two or three gallons. The case was placed in a bag, and taken to the customers by a woman in the service. When the place was entered by the officers of the law, a large quantity of material and all the appliances employed in the manufacture of whisky were found.[42]

Following the defeat of Napoleon in 1815, the British economy soon moved into depression – no longer supported by high government spending and the lack of foreign competition. The Excise Act of October 1814 abolished the system of still licences according to capacity and fixed the fee at £10 per annum. It also restored the old system of taxing wash and spirits and – crucial for the Highland distillers – fixed the minimum (legal) still capacity in the Highlands at 500 gallons. To add insult to injury, a move by the Scottish Excise Board to allow for smaller stills in the Highlands and to remove the previous bar upon Highland distillers selling their product in the Lowlands was blocked in the Court of Session by the Lowland distillers. Legal distilling above the Highland Line all but ceased: in 1816, there were only 12 entered distilleries in the Highlands. The smugglers had a heyday.

'The consequence [of this Act] was ruin to many respectable distillers,' wrote Samuel Morewood, a Collector of Excise in Ireland and the author of a seminal work on 'Inebriating Liquors', published in 1824, 'as well as great injury to the revenue by the production and smuggling of Highland whisky – a liquor, which, from its mildness and good flavour, was more consonant to the tastes and habits of the Scotch people.'[43]

Together with the maltsters and the licensed Highland distillers, the landed interest in Scotland pressed the new chairman of the Scottish Excise Board, Major Woodbine Parish of Bawburgh Old Hall, to reduce duty (as a way of combating the smugglers), reduce the required size of still (to encourage more distillers to 'enter') and to allow for weaker washes (which would improve the quality of the spirit). Highland landowners agreed that if these demands were met they would foster the licensed trade and help suppress smuggling.

The result was the Small Stills Act of 1816, which abolished the Highland Line and allowed stills of no less than 40 gallons capacity throughout Scotland (subject to persons applying for a licence being recommended by two magistrates and their parish minister). It also reduced spirits duty to 8s 4d (the following year this was further reduced to 5s 6d). The number of licensed distilleries in the Highlands rose from 12 to 36 and when an Amending Act was passed in 1818, which at last allowed weaker washes, the number rose to 57.

The Bard and the Bottle

David Purdie

> O Whisky, soul o'plays and pranks!
> Accept a Bardie's gratefu' thanks,
> When lacking thee, what tuneless cranks
> Are my poor verses!
> Thou comes, and they rattle i' their ranks
> At ither's arses!

Thus, in his early poem 'Scotch Drink', does Scotland's greatest bard and songwriter pay earthy tribute to his muse's spirituous liberation by whisky. He personifies the spirit in many of his works, as 'John Barleycorn', or hails it as 'thou king o' grain'.

Later in 'Scotch Drink' he takes a swipe at 'The cursed horse-leeches o' the Excise, wha mak the whisky Stills their Prize'. There is delightful irony here since just a few years later the bard himself would be a 'horse-leech' as an officer of the excise service, forerunner of our beloved HMRC.

It was also Mr Barleycorn who infused raw courage into the eponymous hero of Burns's masterpiece 'Tam o' Shanter'. The tipsy farmer rides home through a storm from a whisky-fuelled carousal with his chums after a market in Ayr. He then blunders into a warlocks and witches' coven and dance going full blast in the haunted Kirk of Alloway. Is he affrighted? Not a bit of it!

> Inspiring bold John Barleycorn!
> What dangers thou canst make us scorn!
> Wi' tippeny, we fear nae evil;   [beer]
> Wi' usquabae, we'll face the devil!   [whisky]

John Barleycorn was also the necessary pseudonym used by Exciseman Burns in a poetical address to the Prime Minister himself on the vexed question of taxation. His 'Address of the Scottish Distillers to the Right Hon. William Pitt' appeared in the *Edinburgh Evening Courant* in February 1789. It followed the imposition of the Scotch Distillery Act (1786) and the ruination, claims the poet, '...by a positive breach of the Public Faith, in a most partial

Right.
Robert Burns, 1759–1796. Poet by Alexander Nasmyth.

Overleaf.
The inauguration of Robert Burns as Poet Laureate of the Lodge by William Stewart Watson, 1846.

tax by the House of Commons, to favour a few opulent English Distillers who, it seems, were of vast Electioneering consequence'. The Scotch whisky industry had thus been 'sacrificed, without remorse, to the infernal deity of political expediency'.

This was not the first time that Burns had unsheathed his pen like a rapier in defence of the distillers of Caledonia. The 'Author's earnest Cry & Prayer to the Rt Hon. and Hon. Scotch Representatives in the House of Commons' is a witty plea to the 45 Scots MPs to do their duty by obtaining a fair duty on Scotch. Burns's hilarious description of the effect on his muse of the current whisky dearth shows him at his humorous best:

> Alas! My roupet Muse is hoarse!   [croaky]
> Your Honours' hearts wi' grief 'twad pierce
> To see her sitting on her Arse,
> Low i' the Dust,
> And screechin' out prosaic Verse,
> An' like to burst!

It can already be seen that the relationship between Scotland's national bard and her national drink is both intimate and complex. As such it is highly instructive both in terms of Burns's biography and the place of *uisge beatha*, the 'water of life', in the eighteenth-century society he inhabited.

Burns mixed easily with both the gentry and the commonality, enjoying the claret and port of the former as much as the whisky of the latter. In a letter to his farmer friend John Tennant from Auchenbay, who had sent him a cask of whisky, Burns writes:

> My Dear Sir,
> I yesterday tried my cask of whisky for the first time, and I assure you it does you great credit... The whisky of this country is a most rascally liquor; and, by consequence, only drunk by the most rascally part of the inhabitants.
>   A neighbour of mine, John Currie... he and his wife... keep a country public-house & sell a great deal of foreign spirits, but all along thought that whisky would have degraded their house. They were perfectly astonished at my whisky, both for its taste and strength...

Whisky may indeed have begun as a raw 'rascally liquor' for the poorest sectors of society, but in the hands of such as Johnny Tennant improvement was underway. However, Burns's grave would be green for over 25 years before the Excise Act of 1823 allowed previously illegal stills to be licensed. A year later the Glenlivet was the first single malt to go on sale legally and the international success of the great array of our blends and single malts would have been a matter of pride for the bard.

An anonymous obituary in the Edinburgh papers of July 1796 alleged that, at the age of just 37, Robert Burns had died of drink. It is now known that the author was a man who never met him and that the actual cause of his premature death was endocarditis, not John Barleycorn. However, the mud stuck and in any short essay touching on Burns and alcohol the record needs to be set straight. Our poet was no teetotaller but like all sensible men his enjoyment of grape and grain was confined to the evening social hours with his friends. Never did he let it interfere with his domestic responsibilities to Jean Armour Burns and their children, nor to his professional duties for the excise or the Royal Dumfries Volunteers, in which regiment he was serving.

The final toast, however, must be to the juice of the barley itself. Like Burns's poems and songs themselves, whisky is one of Scotland's many contributions to the weal and welfare of mankind. 'John Barleycorn — a Ballad' is derived, the poet tells us in his Commonplace Book, from old folksongs describing the ancient Corn Spirit and hailing whisky as the glorious offspring of the barley. The song follows the process of whisky-making, from the harvest field to the final emergence of the spirit, and ends:

> Then let us toast John Barleycorn,
> And may his great posterity
> Ne'er fail in Old Scotland!

Amen to that.

VI
Carrot and Stick

'The law is out of harmony with a great body of public opinion, for whom it has lost respect'

Evidence from an excise officer to *The Fifth Commission of Inquiry into the Revenue*

The years that followed Waterloo and the end of the Napoleonic Wars were a time of general discontent and turmoil. The demands of war, which had stimulated industrial production, gave way to economic depression and unemployment, exacerbated by the return of thousands of de-mobilised servicemen. The cost of living had risen sharply towards the end of the war, as had the population (owing to a better diet and medical discoveries such as inoculation against smallpox), while the price of grain plummeted, bankrupting many farmers. Starvation, malnourishment and despair were endemic.

Lord Liverpool's Tory government was determined to remain firm, resolved to defend the interests of the landed class, which kept it in power. The fear was that the many local agitations, rick-burnings and machine-breakings that had sprung up all over the country were part of a great conspiracy and that if they gave an inch there would be no knowing where it might end. There being no police force, the army was frequently called out to break up local agitations – most famously in 1819 at St Peter's Fields, Manchester, the so-called 'Peterloo Massacre'.

The following year the 'Cato Street Conspiracy' was uncovered, revealing a plan to assassinate the Cabinet during a dinner party in Grosvenor Square. Two months later the three supposed leaders of an insurrection in Scotland, which had been swiftly crushed at Bonnymuir near Stirling, were hanged, then beheaded as traitors before a huge mob.

Landowners were becoming increasingly nervous. Here was anarchy staring them in the face: if smugglers could bring the excise laws into disrepute, all laws might be brought into disrepute. At the same time, many landowners began to see clear possibilities of profiting by becoming distillers themselves, or by securing licences for legal distilling on their estates. But this would only happen if smuggling could be suppressed, the burden of duty lightened and the mass of tax regulations rationalised.

Nonetheless, widespread smuggling continued, and Justices of the Peace still tended to be lenient. In 1819, more than a quarter of the 4,201 cases heard in magistrates courts were dismissed. Alfred Barnard, editor of the licensed trade journal *Harper's Weekly Gazette,* supplies a good example from Campbeltown:

The Peterloo Massacre of 1819.

A capital story is told of an aged woman who resided near Hazelburn [Kintyre]. She was of a rather doubtful character and was charged before the Sheriff with smuggling. The charge being held proven, it fell to his lordship to pronounce sentence. When about to do so he thus addressed the culprit:

'I daresay my poor woman it is not often you have been guilty of this fault.'

'Deed no Sheriff,' she readily replied, 'I haena made a drap since yon wee keg I sent to yersel.'[44]

There were inconclusive debates in parliament about the smuggling problem. Alexander, 4th Duke of Gordon, one of the largest landowners in Scotland, whose estates included the notorious smuggling districts of Glenlivet and the Cabrach, became the spokesman for the landed interest. In 1820 he urged the

House of Lords to extend the policies introduced by the Acts of 1816 and 1818 in order to make it possible for small distillers to make good whisky and sell it at a reasonable profit. In return, he pledged the support of landowners in suppressing illicit distilling by evicting tenants who had been convicted.

William P. Coyne, Superintendent of Statistics and Intelligence at the Department of Agriculture and Technical Instruction for Ireland, summed up the situation retrospectively: 'In the year 1820 illicit distillation had become so prevalent in the United Kingdom, that more than half of the spirits actually consumed were supplied by the smuggler, and it was found necessary to appoint a Parliamentary Commission to investigate the subject, and propose a remedy.'[45]

The aforementioned Commission of Inquiry into the Revenue was set up the following year under the chairmanship of Thomas Wallace, later Lord Wallace, vice-president of the Board of Trade. Meanwhile the Illicit Distillation (Scotland) Act 1822 dramatically raised the penalties associated with possessing and using un-gauged stills, and conveying illicit spirits. Landowners who sanctioned illicit distilling could be fined and the discretionary power of magistrates to reduce fines in cases of hardship was removed. Excisemen were permitted to remove or destroy equipment without a warrant from the Justices of the Peace.

It soon became apparent to the commissioners that the smugglers had a virtual monopoly of the whisky trade in the Highlands and that their product was so well thought of that many Lowland distillers found it worthwhile to buy

A distiller at work. Illustration from *The Art of Distillation*, 1651.

up quantities and re-sell it under their own names. As Sillett writes in *Illicit Scotch*:

> The truth of the matter was that smuggled spirits at from six to seven shillings a gallon, twenty-two degrees over-proof [70% ABV], represented an infinitely better buy than legally distilled raw grain spirits at eight shillings a gallon, or malt spirits at nineteen shillings and sixpence, both at seven degrees over-proof [61% ABV], which was the highest strength at which legal distillers could sell their spirits.

Captain William Fraser of Brackla, who had founded his distillery on the Cawdor Estate near Nairn in 1812, told the Commission that although Brackla was the only licensed distillery between Inverness and Aberdeen, 'he had not sold 100 gallons for consumption within 120 miles of his residence during the past year, though people drank nothing but whisky'.

His friend, Captain Hugh Munro, founder of Teaninich Distillery at Alness, Ross-shire, complained that while he had a warehouse on-site holding 4,000 gallons of whisky, there was not a local customer to be had. James Haig, owner of three distilleries in Edinburgh and the leading spokesman for the Lowland distillers, deponed that his consignments to the Aberdeen market in 1822 amounted to only 'two or three puncheons', where it had been 100 to 150 only a few years before.

An excise official summed up the situation: 'The law is out of harmony with a great body of public opinion, for whom it has lost respect.'

The Wallace Commission reported its findings in 1823, at a time when the government was yielding to the need for reform in a variety of areas. Lord Liverpool's Chancellor of the Exchequer, 'Prosperity' Robinson, welcomed the findings since they would add to the revenue and were in tune with the administration's desire to rationalise the Trade Laws. The commission's recommendations were embodied in the 1823 Excise Act – a measure which laid the foundations of the modern whisky industry.

This key Act set the licence fee for distilling at £10 per annum. Duty was more than halved (to 2s 5d a gallon of spirits made) and a rebate or drawback of 1s 5d per gallon was allowed for spirits made with malt – a sop to Highland distillers since malt was more expensive (the large Lowland distillers mainly used other cereals). The right to use stills as small as 40 gallons was continued, and thin washes allowed, to increase the quality of the spirit. At the same time, in terms of the Illicit Distillation (Scotland) Act 1822, the Board of Excise was duty-bound to put an end to smuggling, with military support if required, and gaugers were empowered to enter premises without warrant.

The result of the new regulations was a steep increase in the quantity of

An illicit Highland still by moonlight.

legally made spirits. In 1820, in the United Kingdom (including Ireland), 9.6 million gallons were distilled; by 1826, this figure was 18.2 million gallons. But the provisions of the Act were deeply resented in the Highlands. The crofters and small farmers considered themselves to be law-abiding people, notwithstanding their attitude to the laws relating to smuggling, and claimed they were deserving of better treatment than the bands of desperados operating in the vicinity of Glasgow, Stirling and Perth.

Smuggling, on a large scale, continued in spite of the Act. In the Elgin Collection district alone, there were 3,061 detections of illicit distilling or malting, without giving notice in the year ending 5 July 1824. The collector estimated that there were more than 400 small stills at work in the area embracing the Cabrach, Glenrinnes and Glenlivet, and that an average of 300 bolls of barley a week were transported into the district in the autumn of 1823. He hinted that what he needed was a troop of cavalry to enforce the law.

Former smugglers who 'went legal', such as George Smith in Glenlivet, were often threatened by their former colleagues, considered 'traitors to the cause', and in some cases had their newly licensed distilleries burnt to the ground. A tenant of the Duke of Gordon, Smith was the first distiller in the region we now know as Speyside to take out a licence. In 1823, he had taken over the joint tenancy of Upper Drimmin Farm on the understanding that he would establish an 'entered' distillery there. In the 1860s he wrote to the *London Scotsman* newspaper:

[W]hen the new Act was heard of, both in Glenlivet and in the Highlands of Aberdeenshire, they [i.e. the illicit distillers] ridiculed the

Right.
Lochnagar Distillery on Deeside which, following the visit of Victoria and Albert in 1849, became Royal Lochnagar Distillery.

Below.
Corgarff Castle in Donside. Following the Jacobite rising of 1745, it and Braemar Castle on Deeside were occupied by Government Forces. It has been suggested that in addition to their military duties, the occupying garrisons were enthusiastic customers for locally produced spirit.

ROYAL LOCHNAGAR DISTILLERY.

idea that anyone would be found daring enough to commence legal distilling in their midst. The proprietors [i.e. the landowners] were very anxious to fulfil their pledge to the Government and did everything they could to encourage the commencement of legal distillation; but the desperate character of the smugglers and the violence of their threats deterred anyone for some time.

The lookout was an ugly one . . . I was warned before I began by my civil neighbours that they meant to burn the distillery to the ground, and me at the heart of it. The laird of Aberlour presented me with a pair of hair-trigger pistols worth ten guineas, and they were never out of my belt for ten years.

I got together two or three stout fellows for servants, armed them with pistols, and let it be known everywhere that I would fight for my place till the last shot. I had a pretty good character as a man of my word, and through watching, by turns, every night for years, we contrived to save the distillery from the fate so freely predicted for it.

But I often, both at kirk and market, had rough times of it among the glen people and if had not been for the laird of Aberlour's pistols, I don't think I should be telling you this story now.[46]

The fear of reprisals from smugglers was no mere paranoia. George Smith mentions that three more small distilleries took out licences in Glenlivet in 1825–26, 'but the smugglers succeeded very soon in frightening away their occupants, none of whom ventured to hang on a single year in the face of the threats uttered so freely against them'. Banks O'Dee Distillery, Aberdeen, was burnt down by smugglers in 1825. In June the same year, two of George Smith's brothers were charged with assaulting an excise officer 'when making a private distillery detection' near their brother's new licensed distillery. The first Lochnagar Distillery, established on Deeside in 1826, disappeared in a cloud of smoke and suspicious circumstances some years later.

'The country was in a desperately lawless state at this time,' continues George Smith. 'The riding officers of the revenue were a mere sport of the smugglers, and nothing was more common than for them to be shown a still at work, and then coolly defied to make a seizure.'

Indeed, between 1824 and 1830 there seems to have been a brief but vigorous resurgence in illicit distilling. Military garrisons were stationed in several places to support the excise service, not least at Corgarff Castle in Upper Strathdon, to police the unruly Cabrach and Glenlivet. Corgarff is a stark tower protected by a star-shaped perimeter wall and set in open moorland. In 1571, it was burnt by Adam Gordon of Auchindoun in Glenfiddich, together with its 27 residents. It was restored soon after the 1745 Jacobite Rising and garrisoned, rented to a local farmer in 1802 then re-garrisoned in 1827, with no fewer than two officers and 56 men of the 25th Foot regiment for four years.

But there were brave souls who, like George Smith, 'werna fleggit', and social attitudes were changing in their favour.

Smuggling was on the decline. Convictions in magistrates' courts fell from 4,563 in 1823 to 873 in 1825. They continued to decline steadily each subsequent year, to 85 in 1832, with courts in most areas imposing heavier fines (Elgin and Aberdeenshire were exceptions). Colonel Alexander Campbell, a Commissioner of Excise, reported in 1830 that 'illicit distillation and private malting . . . are in a great many parts quite abolished' and that some former smugglers had taken up weaving.[47]

A letter in the *Inverness Courier*, dated 13 January 1830, reminds us that illicit distilling was not wholly extirpated:

> It is a notorious fact that the officers of excise have not succeeded in eradicating smuggling, although they have hunted the offenders against the Excise Laws from glen to glen . . . It is equally notorious that the spirit distilled by the smugglers is infinitely more wholesome, of a finer flavour, and in every way more highly prized than the licensed whisky.

There were some who regretted the passing of the small stills, as witnessed by a letter in the same newspaper dated 4 April 1831:

> It is asserted that the rage for the use of whisky is still increasing, while to our sad experience we know that its quality is deteriorating among us. It is no longer the pure dew of the mountain which issued from the bothies of our free traders of the hills, healthful and as exhilarating as the drops which the sun's first rays drink up from the heathbell of the Cairngorms, but a vile, rascally, mixed compotation which fires the blood and maddens the veins without warming the heart, or, like the old, elevating the understanding.

During the 1830s, '40s and early '50s vast quantities of spirits were drunk in Scotland, and with whisky taxed at 3/4d a gallon since 1823 most people could afford to drink to their heart's content. For the working classes, illicit spirits supplemented legal whisky. Of the 700 detections of illicit stills in 1833–35, many were now found in the sprawling slums of cities. John Dunlop, a magistrate in Greenock, wrote, 'in no other country does spirituous liquid seem to have assumed so much the attitude of the authorized instrument of compliment and kindness as in North Britain'.[48]

The drinks trade journal *Harper's Manual* estimated that: 'In the 1830s, the

Carrot and Stick

Excisemen and civic dignitaries proudly pose with illicit distilling equipment seized in Glasgow.

population [of Scotland] aged fifteen and over was drinking, on average, the equivalent of a little under a pint each of duty-charged whisky a week.'[49] By 1835 Glasgow had one licence holder or public house for every 14 families.

The editor of *The Scotsman*, who was not alone in his concern about the amount of whisky being drunk in Scotland, commented: 'Glasgow was three times more drunken than Edinburgh, and five times more so than London.'[50]

Although smuggling had declined, it was still a problem that the customs and excise services failed to solve, to the significant detriment of the Exchequer. The 1840s was a period of severe economic depression and, when he became Prime Minister in 1841, Sir Robert Peel was confronted with a budget deficit of £7.5 million. His solutions were radical. First, he reintroduced income tax, at a rate of seven pence in the pound, on incomes over £150 per annum [£12,600 in today's money] as a temporary measure.[51] The money raised, which was more than expected, allowed him to address ways to increase revenue from customs and excise – not by increasing duties but by reducing or abolishing them.

In this he was following William Pitt's example. Peel believed that lowering duties would stimulate the economy and encourage more people to buy dutiable goods; he was also sceptical about the effectiveness of collection. In 1843 he remarked, 'I confess I distrust everything about the Customs [Service], so far as to feel assured that a vast many [officers] have been dishonest and none have been vigilant.'[52] During his ministry he abolished or reduced duty on more than 1,200 items, mainly imports, and including, in 1846, those on imported grain (the repeal of the Corn Laws), which challenged the landed interest – traditional supporters of the Tory Party – and brought down the government.

Almost all the malt whisky made during the middle decades of the nineteenth century – legally and illegally – was drunk in Scotland.

Overleaf.
The Illicit Highland Whisky Still, by Sir Edwin Landseer c.1829.

As the unnamed journalist mentioned above reported to *Harper's Manual* in 1915, referring to 'the year his parents visited the Great Exhibition' (i.e. 1851)[53]:

> In our early school-days at 'Auld Reekie' whisky was an all but unknown quantity beyond the confines of Scotland itself. On the southern side of the Border it was scarcely to be had, certainly not of fine quality. Scotsmen travelling to various parts of England took their supplies along with them, paying half-a-crown per gallon extra Excise duty at Berwick-on-Tweed, or, if by steamboat or sailing vessel, on landing at their destination.[54]

Most patent-still grain whisky went to England for rectification into gin, and some was sold cheaply as 'British Spirits'. The rest was drunk in Scotland, sometimes mixed with malt whisky by licensed grocers.

Sir Robert Usher recollected in 1908: 'Before 1860 very little Scotch whisky was sent to England for sale [i.e. as such], but after that year trade in Scotch whisky increased by leaps and bounds.' His contention was supported by Winston Churchill, himself a keen whisky drinker (Johnnie Walker Black Label was his favourite): 'My father would never have tasted Scotch, except on a moor or some other damp and dreary place. His generation drank brandy.'

Sir Robert's father, Andrew Usher, is credited with being the first person to create a blend of malt and grain whiskies which was consistent batch on batch, and which could therefore be branded: Usher's Old Vatted Glenlivet. This was in 1853 and was probably a mix of malt whiskies, which was allowed before duty had to be paid. Other licensed grocers began to do the same and when, in 1860, Gladstone's Spirits Act permitted the mixing of malt with grain whisky under bond, blended Scotch soon became the norm.

As early as 1864, Charles Tovey was able to write: 'The prevalent notion among whisky drinkers, especially in Scotland, is that several varieties of whisky blended is superior to that of any one kind'.[55]

It might be claimed with some justification that the success of blended Scotch whisky sounded the death-knell of illicit distilling. In 1864 there were only 19 detections of illicit stills; ten years later there were six. With blending, flavour could be 'designed' to suit the palates of non-Scottish drinkers – in other words, to have a far broader appeal. It could also be made to be consistent from batch to batch and could therefore be branded and widely promoted to markets which could now be reached easily by the extensive rail network that covered the country.

The whisky trade became an industry, and illicit distilling and smuggling a romantic memory recalled in music, song and legend, as well as paintings by Victorian artists such as Sir Edwin Landseer.

VII
The Last Gasps

'A [final] violent and sustained outburst of smuggling'

Ian Macdonald, *Smuggling in the Highlands*

There was a revival of 'those pernicious habits which had in the past led to so much lawlessness, dishonesty, idleness and drinking' during the 1880s. As Ian Macdonald writes, it was a 'violent and sustained outburst of smuggling which was not only serious as regards the Revenue and licensed traders, but threatened to demoralise and impoverish the communities and districts affected'.[56]

Macdonald, a retired officer of the Inland Revenue, ascribed the reasons for this to three factors: the abolition of the Malt Tax in 1880, the reduction in the number of excise officers, and the security of tenure provided by the Crofters' Act.

He further remarked: 'The fear of being removed from their holdings has had much influence in limiting illicit distillation.'

Prior to 1880, the malting of barley by unlicensed traders was illegal. Since the process lasts between 14 and 20 days (depending on the weather) and involves steeping, germinating and drying the malt, unlicensed maltsters were perilously open to detection during this period of time. With the removal of this constraint, illicit distilling could only be detected while brewing and distilling. The difficulties of detection were compounded by 'the indiscriminate reduction of the Preventative Force in the Highlands immediately prior to 1880'.

The Crofters' Holdings (Scotland) Act 1886 defined the terms 'crofter' and 'crofting parish', granted security of land tenure to crofters and the right to bequeath their holdings, and created the Crofters' Commission, a land court which ruled on disputes between landlords and crofting tenants. The Act was a direct response to increasing restlessness in the Highlands and Islands, owing to landlords clearing their estates of tenants to make way first for sheep and later for deer forests, both of which were more economically viable than small farms. In the early 1880s the Highland Land League was formed, closely modelled on the Irish Land League of 1878, to draw attention to the crofters' lack of secure tenure and radically reduced access to land. Demands for reform were backed by direct action – rent strikes and land raids (the occupation of land which had been given over to sheep or deer) – notably on Skye, where 'the Battle of the Braes' was supressed by 50 police officers, later replaced by 400 marines to maintain law and order.

As had happened during the Jacobite era, illicit distilling by a new genera-

Battle of the Braes

tion of younger and more rebellious crofters increased, albeit on a small and local scale. Smuggling was once again socially acceptable in the Highlands, even an honourable rejection of unjust laws, landlords and a remote government. In 1884, there were 22 detections, the highest total for over a decade, mainly in the northern crofting counties.

Substantial illicit enterprises were discovered at Alligin, Wester Ross, in 1886. The following year a 'preventative station' was set up by the Excise at Bonar Bridge to patrol the district. Within weeks they found a large still not far from the main road between Ardgay and Dingwall. 'This was no small scale operation; the Excisemen found two mash tuns, one capable of holding 350 gallons, the other 250, plus fermenting tuns of sixty gallons and a whole collection of equipment which would not have been out of place in a legal distillery ... There were also extensive piles of draff, which revealed that it had been in operation for some time.'[57]

Later the same month, they found ten small stills hidden in the hills and surprised a band of smugglers moving their equipment from one bothy to another.

A Commission of Enquiry chaired by Francis, Lord Napier had been set up in 1883, but its report the following year fell a long way short of addressing the crofters' demands and only served to stimulate further protests. Many

The Last Gasps

An early nineteenth-century sketch by Landseer of a simple, rustic distilling operation.

thousands of crofters joined the Highland Land League and its political wing, the Crofters' Party, and in the general election of 1885, five Crofters' Party MPs were returned to Westminster.

Although the Crofters' Holdings Act became known as 'the Magna Carta of Gaeldom' it did not quell the agitation, largely owing to the inability of the Crofters Commission to resolve disputes between landlords and tenants, although the incidence of illicit distilling seems to have subsided once again. Steve Sillett writes, 'Excise seizures in the 1900s – of which there were many – were almost entirely in respect of small stills and other essential brewing and distilling utensils which had long been abandoned by their owners. Over the years 1907 to 1908, only one detection was made in respect of illicit distilling.'[58]

In 1909, a second Highland Land League was formed in Glasgow with a clear left-wing political agenda, including the restoration of deer forests to public ownership, the nationalisation of the land and home rule for Scotland. In the general election of 1918, four joint Labour–Land League MPs were returned.[59]

Post-Great War excise duty increases stimulated illicit distilling. 'By 1934, illicit distillation was sufficiently widely practised as to present a serious threat to the interests of the legitimate distiller, Revenue and taxpayer alike', writes Malcolm Archibald in *Whisky Wars, Riots and Murder*, 'a state of affairs which

Excise officer Murdoch Mackenzie, in kilt, and two of his men with a confiscated illicit still near Gairloch.

demanded decisive action on the part of the Courts in making scape-goats of offenders brought before them.' Some draconian sentences were handed down, both custodial and monetary. For example, a number of smugglers in Gairloch who were caught red-handed in their bothy were summarily imprisoned, while another band in the remote Kilsyth Hills, who had been conducting a lucrative trade in Glasgow and who were also caught in the act of distilling, opted to go to prison rather than pay the onerous fines imposed upon them.

But the glory days of smuggling were long gone. There may still be small stills being operated in Scotland, mainly in urban situations, according to Her Majesty's Revenue & Customs, but HMRC have more pernicious fish to fry – drugs, tobacco, derivatives of endangered animal species (reptile skins, ivory, tortoise shells, coral, rare parrots) – and, increasingly, asylum seekers fleeing war zones or in search of economic betterment, some of whom finish up as household slaves or prostitutes.

As Malcolm Archibald put it: 'There is still illicit whisky being made in the Highlands, but not on anything like the scale of the nineteenth century. The old days of smugglers rising en masse against the excisemen or ambushing them with muskets are in the past and history has cast a romantic gloss over those days. Now whisky is a major legal industry and a large employer. Times have changed.'

The Dram in Folklore

Tom McKean

Whisky — a key ingredient in Scottish culture – is used to celebrate births, courtship and marriage; to mark a death, a sporting victory; to drown the agony of defeat; to celebrate life. Little wonder, then, that whisky and the making of it plays a substantial role in the mythologies of Scotland and in its song and musical culture. Examples abound: Neil Gow's 'Farewell to Whisky' and 'Welcome Whisky Back Again', the song 'Nancy Whiskey' and Stanley Robertson's 'The Merchant's Son', in which strong drink leads to a young man losing his sense, his money and his clothing:

> Intae the mornin the wench rose
> An she's put on the merchant's clothes
> His cap sae high an his sword sae clear
> She bung avree wi the gadgie's gear.
>
> [went away; non-Traveller]

In Gaelic culture, too, whisky looms large, with songs such as 'Thug an t-Uisge-beatha Sin an Car Asam A-raoir' ('The Whisky Tricked Me Last Night') and 'Caraid is Nàmhaid an Uisge-bheatha' ('The Friend and the Enemy of Whisky'), a debate in song about the virtues and demerits of the stuff. Many of these songs conflate the influence of women and whisky on the poor hapless male of the species, a powerlessness perhaps best reflected in a wee Gaelic story which tells of 'Smeòrach ag Ràdh ri Duine am Botal Uisge-bheatha Aige Òl' ('A Thrush Telling a Man to Drink his Bottle of Whisky'), surely the poorest excuse ever offered to a long-suffering wife.

In contrast with these tunes and songs of celebration, victimhood and apology, there are those which tell in excoriating detail of the effects

Whisky quaichs and other eighteenth-century drinking vessels.

drink can have on domestic life, such as Robertson's 'Johnnie, My Man':

> Johnnie, my man, oor bairnies are aa greetin
> Nae meal in the barrel tae fill their
>   wee wames   [stomachs]
> While ye sit here a-drinkin,
>   you leave me lamenting
> Arise up, my Johnnie, an come awa hame.

Within these testaments to the cultural impact of drink, both positive and negative, is a subcategory of songs to do with the (usually illicit) making of the stuff. Perhaps the best known of these is 'The Yowie wi the Crookit Horn', ostensibly about a missing sheep but actually about the stealing of an illicit still, the 'crookit horn' being the coil, the 'worm' the device itself, as sung by Elizabeth Stewart on *Up Yon Wide and Lonely Glen: Travellers' Songs, Stories and Tunes of the Fetterangus Stewarts*:

> My yowie wi the crookit horn,
>   my yowie wi the crookit horn   [ewe]
> Oh siccan a yowie ne'er wis born;
>   she's teen fae me an teen awa.
>   [such a ewe; taken]

> Peer wee thing for aa my keepin,
>   there came a nickum fin I wis sleepin
>   [Poor; little devil]
> There came a nickum fin I wis sleepin an
>   took my yowie, horn an aa.

The hapless distiller is beside himself.

> If I hid the lad that did it, I wid sweir
>   by the lad that said it
> Though the laird himsel he should forbit it,
>   I'd gie tae him his neck a thraw.   [twist]

Sometimes, of course, a sheep is just a sheep; the song was remade by Rev. John Skinner in a version that is clearly about an ovine, rather than a copper, beast.

Neil Gow, the legendary eighteenth-century fiddler, by Sir Henry Raeburn.

A lesser-known song, from the Gaelic tradition, is 'Oran na Poite Duibhe' ('The Black Pot Song'), sung by Finlay Murchison for the American collector James Madison Carpenter in the 1930s, and found in Atlantic Canada in the 1950s as well. The song draws on bovine rather than ovine imagery, but the meaning is still pretty clear.

> Fhuair sinn nuas bho ard Mhic Shimidh
> Bo mhaol dhubh 's i air leth shine
> 'S iomadh fear a thig le sgilinn
> 'G iarraidh dilleag dhe cuid bainne. [...]
>
> 'S tric a thug me fhein a Lòir dhi
> Subh an eorna 's fhearr 's an talamh. [...]
>
> Dhat an ùgh aice le ruaidh
> 'S cha toireadh an laogh boinne uaith
> Chuir sinn teine fo dà chruachan
> 'S theann i air cur uaithe bhainne.
>
> *From the heights of Lovat we got*
> *A black cow with only one teat*
> *Many a man comes with a penny*
> *Wanting a wee drop of her milk.*
>
> *Often I give her her fill*
> *Of the best juice of the barley in the land.*
>
> *Her udder swelled up with inflammation*
> *And the calf couldn't get a drop of milk out*
>   *of her*
> *We put a fire under [her] two hips*
> *And at once she started to give the milk.*

Once the still was running, another concern raised its head, critical to any illicit distiller:

> 'S eagal oirnn gun tig na seoid
> 'S gun fag iad sinn gun bho 's
>   gun bhainne
>
> *We're afraid the heroes [excisemen]*
>   *will come*
> *And that they'd leave us with neither cow*
>   *nor milk*

The authorities, seeing the population enjoying something that they were able to make for themselves, naturally wished to tax and thus control it, and the exciseman was probably the least popular member of the civil service. Robert Burns encapsulated distillers' hopes and attitudes in his inimitable way, suggesting that the devil has met his match:

> The deil cam fiddlin' thro' the town
> And danc'd awa wi' th' Exciseman
> And ilka wife cries, 'Auld Mahoun,
> I wish you luck o' the prize, man.'

Over in North America, Scottish and Irish settlers continued a love affair with whisk(e)y making, and the stories and songs that go with it. In Appalachia, the title 'Give the Fiddler a Dram' speaks of the place of drink in social life, while 'Whiskey before Breakfast' hints at a wry sense of humour and, perhaps, an aspiration to the good life. Songs such as 'Old Whisker Bill, the Moonshiner', recorded in 1927 by Buell Kazee, embody the joie de vivre we associate with the freewheeling scofflaw distiller.

> I've been a moonshiner for seven
>   long years,
> I've spent all my money on whiskey
>   and beers,
>
> I'll go up some dark holler,
>   I'll set up my still,
> I'll still you one gallon for a
>   two dollar bill,
>
> Purty women, purty women,
>   don't trouble my mind,
> If the whiskey don't kill me I'll
>   live a long time.

Whisky and women: an incomparable combination. In the distiller's mind, anyway.

> God bless them pretty women,
>   I wish they all were mine
> Their breath smells so sweetly, like
>   good old moonshine.

In Newfoundland, the terrain was perhaps even more difficult for the authorities to patrol than that of Scotland, with many communities — the outports — accessible only by sea, and even then not for much of the winter. The incentive to home-distil can scarce have been stronger. Even so, distillers lived in fear of both the authorities and a local clype, as in Pat Troy's 'The Moonshine Can', collected by Kenneth Pink in 1959:

> Come all my friends and comrades,
>   come listen unto me,
> Beware of those informers,
>   you see how they served me,
> Beware of those informers,
>   good people all around,
> For jealously could not agree,
>   they put our whisky down.
>
> On Easter Sunday morning as you may
>   plainly see,
> As soon as Mickey got the news he did
>   come down to me,
> He did come down to me, my boys,
>   and put me on a stand,
> Saying, Pat, there is a big kick up about
>   your moonshine can.

The poor man is heartbroken when the still is disposed of:

> Sure I went in and brought it out and
>   that with no delay,
> I stood just like a monument without
>   one word to say,
> To hear those pipes a-rattling it grieved
>   my heart full sore,
> And when he put them in the bay it
>   grieved me ten times more.

But he is unrepentant:

> And now our whisky is put down it
>   does seem rather queer,
> Never mind, my darling boys, they
>   won't stick us on the beer,
> We'll go into a neighbour's house and
>   drink a health all round,
> But no health to those informers who
>   put our whisky down.

Appalachian distillers were just as keen to avoid detection and the taxman, as Roscoe Holcomb sings in 'Moonshiner'.

> I'll go up some dark hollow and get
>   you some booze
> If the revenues don't get me,
>   no money will I lose.

Today, though illicit distilling is not done on anything like the scale it was in the past (or so they say), the idea of moonshining still holds a fascination, as attested by the popularity of Alfred Beddoe's 1953 composition 'Copper Kettle', possibly based on a folk original and covered by such luminaries as Joan Baez and Bob Dylan. After advising on the technical side of not getting caught — 'Don't use no green or rotten wood / They'll get you by the smoke' — the song romanticises the distillers' activities and explicitly alludes to the pride felt in avoiding taxation:

> My daddy, he made whiskey
> My granddaddy, he did too
> We ain't paid no whiskey tax since 1792.

The date refers to the hugely unpopular 1791 tax imposed by the United States government which, though it gave rise to the so-called Whisky Rebellion, was not overturned for more than a decade.

Nevertheless, as is the pattern in most taxation, from the raising of taxes on income or petrol, there is widespread indignation and resistance, protest even, followed by acquiescence and general acceptance. Nowadays, whisky is heavily regulated,

The Deil's Awa' Wi the Exciseman. A late eighteenth-century etching by Robert Bryden.

simultaneously taxed and promoted by different branches of the civil service: excise and tourism. But, above all, there is still a hint of romance — and transgression — about drinking it, about singing nostalgic or metaphorical songs about it, and about its place in Scottish social life and custom, which remains undimmed today. Many a Scotsman and woman look forward to a day when the deil will be awa wi' th' Exciseman, as Burns puts it:

> We'll mak our maut, and we'll brew our drink,
> We'll laugh, sing, and rejoice, man,
> And mony braw thanks to the meikle black deil,
> That danc'd awa wi' th' Exciseman.

Smuggling's Heartland: The Cabrach

Daniel MacCannell

I
A Raiding Base on the Highland Line

'[H]is Majesty's peaceable subjects in the north parts have been grievously infested these diverse years bygone, to the dishonour of God, disgrace of his Majesty's government, and disturbance of the public peace'

Commission to the Marquis of Huntly, 1635

A novel hypothesis worth exploring is that the historical persistence, escalating violence and increasing scale of smuggling activities by members of the Clan Gordon over a period of 200 years, with the barony of Cabrach serving as a principal hideout, can be traced to the Gordons' old and bitter rivalry with the Campbells of Argyll. Certainly by the 1690s, and perhaps as early as 1644, smuggling of alcohol – of any type – could be seen from a Gordon perspective as a principled, and profitable, mode of resistance to a single hated phenomenon encompassing Calvinist religion, Campbell-family domination of Scottish politics and, of course, Ferintosh: the 'horrid Parliament whisky' that was produced legally and tax-free by the Campbells' bosom allies, the Forbeses of Culloden, between 1690 and 1786. In all of this, the Cabrach Gordons' famed abilities as horsemen, horse-breeders and horse-thieves were very much to the fore. The hitherto seemingly unconnected histories of Royalist guerrilla cavalry warfare, Jacobite military and political intrigue, the illicit importation and distribution of French brandy and Dutch gin, and the clandestine distillation and distribution of untaxed whisky were in fact successive phases in a single web of Gordon-led subversive activity that stretched from the wild uplands of Banffshire to the English Channel and beyond.[1]

•

Backlit by the dawn, the undulating, treeless horizon is broken by two dozen dark figures. Their approach, and the gathering light, reveal them as young gentlemen on horseback, dressed in the fashionable attire of the Jacobean age: floppy velvet hats adorned with feathers and pearls, tight-fitting jackets with stripes of many colours and rain-tarnished silver braid. The brown leather of their tight-fitting thigh-high boots and gauntlet gloves is burnished with long use, as is the silver-inlaid chiselled iron of the handles of their rapiers and parrying daggers. They are greeted enthusiastically by a larger number of men and women, some scarcely less well-dressed than the riders, who banter with them as they unload the heavy saddlebags, distribute drink in tall pewter flagons, or scan the hills for any sign of enraged pursuers: kinfolk of the riders' victims in the not-so-distant country of the MacPhersons and Mackintoshes.

Previous pages.
The view from the Buck of Cabrach.

Opposite.
Looking towards the Buck from Redford, Upper Cabrach.

It is seven years since the Union of the Crowns, which saw King James VI of Scots become King of England also, and the Scottish border has officially ceased to exist, its ancient marches renamed the 'Middle Shires' of a new country called Great Britain. But here, far to the north in the Scottish barony of Cabrach, an equally important frontier remains as dangerous as ever. Long before the twenty-first century, the Cabrach will be noted – if at all – as one of the remotest and least populous areas in Europe. But now, in 1610, the treacherous Rhynie–Mortlach road is a great 'highway betwixt the Highlands and Lowlands'; and the cold and desolate land through which it runs has become a key outpost of a Lowland culture still challenged by a militant – and militarily significant – Highland clanship. Tonight the Gordon horsemen, led by their 'captane', Patrick McGillewrich, have taken the fight to the enemy. Less than five years hence, McGillewrich will be condemned as a 'stark thief' and have a huge price placed on his head. But for now, his audacious band of young Gordon lairds[2] and their close allies, the Leiths of Harthill and Edingarach, carry out their raids under colour of public authority.

King James, governing the country by remote control from his newfound palaces in the south of England, has long divided responsibility for the remoter regions of his native Scotland between two mighty lines of aristocrats: the Campbell earls of Argyll in the west and south-west, and the Gordon earls of Huntly in the north-east and north. Their immense territories are poorly defined, with indistinct boundaries both geographically and jurisdictionally. Yet, few pairs of noble families chosen at random could be more different than these two: the first, mostly staunch Presbyterians, Gaelic in culture, and pragmatic masters of devious behind-the-scenes power games; the latter, Roman Catholics of relatively recent Anglo-French derivation, given to futile, and often fatal, frontal attacks on superior forces, sometimes for a nearly abstract point of principle. But Argyll and Huntly are almost equally rich in land, money, and armed men in their thousands; the king, in his wisdom or unwisdom, loves them both equally, with the result – intended or not – that the earls are regularly at each other's throats.

Just 13 miles south-west of here, in 1571, Forbes of Towie's wife Margaret Campbell was roasted alive in her castle of Corgarff by Huntly's brother, Adam Gordon of Auchindoun. By the early 1590s, 'factional violence reached almost epidemic proportions'[3]; and in September 1593, a pitched battle between Gordon cavalry and Campbell-backed Highland raiders was fought in the Granes of the Gauch, an area of the Cabrach immediately adjoining the Gordon laird's own house, in which McGillewrich also lived. The Gordons were victorious – leaving the corpses of 60 Clan Chattan raiders 'feeding the Cabrach swine.'[4] The result clearly showed the individual Lowland horseman's military advantages over his unmounted Highland rival, but the fact that the battle took

Opposite.
A map of the Cabrach by John Thomson, whose *Atlas of Scotland* was published in 1832. The area was one of the most remote and least populated in Europe. It was in this desolate environment that the ideals of Highland clanship and Lowland culture clashed.

place at all was a lesson about the vulnerability of this frontier zone to Campbell incursions. A much larger struggle between the two rival groupings – Clan Chattan again siding with the Campbells – was fought less than ten miles west of Kirkton of Cabrach in October 1594 and is remembered as the Battle of Glenlivet. Despite being heavily outnumbered, by 10,000 to 2,000, the (mostly mounted) men of the Gordon faction again prevailed.

The Cabrach had long been a 'no man's land' between the Highlands and the Lowlands in the most literal sense. In the Middle Ages, when Scotland's various social, economic and linguistic differences coalesced into these two distinctive cultures, the so-called Forest of Cabrach on the border between Moray and Mar had been home only to a succession of lonely individuals: keepers, responsible for guarding the area's self-perpetuating herds of wild horses that belonged (in broad theory) to the Scottish crown. But even these keepers are not heard of after 1452 – perhaps the last wild horse had been tamed and spirited away; and as recently as 1508 there had been no one living in the Cabrach at all. In that year, the Earl of Huntly granted the lesser nobleman James Gordon of Auchmullan[5] the vacant house of 'Geyauche', later known as Geach or Gauch, or sometimes (perhaps in reference to the medieval horse-keepers) 'the Ward'. Under his leadership, the area's population began to grow. George Gordon, laird of Lesmoir Castle on the Cabrach's eastern fringes, was granted the Cabrach lands of Powneed, Whitehillock, Aldivalloch and Largue in April 1573. By July, he was stealing horses on Upper Deeside and bringing them back to his Cabrach hideout to graze.[6]

One turbulent generation and countless Highland raids later, the Cabrach

Wild and windswept – the Cabrach landscape.

had been subdivided into no fewer than 21 properties, an astonishing ten of them occupied by men of noble birth.[7] Moreover, at a time when many north-east families took the surname Gordon simply to gain the Earl of Huntly's favour or protection, several of the Cabrach's Gordons were the earl's blood kin. Some of the barony's young swordsmen had small landed estates of their own elsewhere in the country; others were younger sons with no land beyond what the earl could offer them here in 'Scotland's Siberia'. But it is remarkable to find so many high-status individuals concentrated within such a confined and agriculturally unproductive area: described in the same period as 'nothing but deaf Rocks, Dens of wild Beasts, and the Fowls of Heaven ... inhospitable, always covered over with Frost and Snow.'[8] The young bloods' presence clearly indicates the Cabrach's continuing strategic importance to the House of Huntly, as well as its suitability for horse-breeding. Scotland was notoriously cash-poor in the early seventeenth century. Yet, in 1610 – at a time when most rents in the north-east were paid in grain, manual labour, cloth, and even live sheep and hens – the 'farmers' of Cabrach collectively paid 366 silver merks per year, a sum equivalent to somewhere between £103,000 and £718,000 today. The occupants' high social status notwithstanding, only some high-value activity, perhaps at the outer limits of legality, could explain the size of this sum – or why a sum *of money* was required of them at all.

Whisky existed at this time, but it was still exclusively a product of the Gaelic west. Distilling, probably of brandy- and gin-like potions, had been introduced in the later fifteenth century by the Scottish arm of the Roman Catholic Church. As that institution slowly declined over the next half-century, the art spread: first to the urban commercial classes, and eventually to the population at large. Certainly, it must have been practised by many different types of people in 1579, when a piece of national legislation (designed to address food shortages) forbade home distillation to all but the gentry and aristocracy for ten months. But as late as the end of the reign of James VI and I, who died in 1625, whisky as we know it was made in the Highlands only. Historical mentions of it become common only in 1610, and references to it being drunk by the upper and middle classes commence only in 1618 – almost inevitably in contexts associated with Clan Campbell.

It would not be stretching a point to suggest that the longer a rivalry continues, however deadly it might be, the more the antagonists will come to resemble one another. A daughter of the earl of Argyll had even married the son and heir of the Earl of Huntly in 1607, as part of a failed initiative to end the enmity between the two power blocs. More importantly, perhaps, Huntly was deeply involved in central government projects to 'civilise' Scotland's west coast: including the creation of Lowland colonies known as 'plantations' on the isles of Lewis, Uist, Barra, Raasay, Rum, Eigg, Canna and St Kilda (though only

A working distillery of 1738 with its various accoutrements.

the first was actually carried out). However ill-conceived or short-lived, such adventures always bring fresh knowledge to those who undertake them. As such, it would be far-fetched to suppose that the House of Gordon would still have been unacquainted with Highland whisky by the time the Plantation of Lewis definitively failed in 1610. Despite being heavily militarised, the Cabrach frontier zone between the Gordon and Campbell spheres of influence was not always militarily active; and in its more idle periods – as with all garrisons everywhere – relief from boredom, or fear, would have been sought in drink. Bought or stolen, then, Highland whisky's high road into Lowland high society in the late Jacobean period could have been, and probably was, via the discerning palates of 'Young Lesmoir', 'Young Harthill', Gordon of Cocklarachie and Captain McGillewrich's other highly born Cabrach lawmen-cum-thieves.

By the mid-1630s, in a curious prefiguration of the classical cowboy film,

A Raiding Base on the Highland Line

The Marquis of Argyll, by David Scougall (c.1610–80).

the Cabrach posse – its leadership now taken over by Alexander Leith, of the Harthill family – would fall victim to the same 'civilising' forces that had brought it into existence in the first place. Leith, along with Gordon of Beldornie's son James, Gordon of Letterfourie's nephew William Ross, 26 other Gordons and 14 other men, 'all in Cabrach', were formally accused of being

> the authors and committers of the many slaughters, fire-raisings . . . and other barbarous oppressions, wherewith his Majesty's peaceable subjects in the north parts have been grievously infested these diverse years bygone, to the dishonour of God, disgrace of his Majesty's government, and disturbance of the public peace[.][9]

In the absence of either a police force or a standing army, arresting these newly

The Netherbow Port, which formed the east gate of the Old Town of Edinburgh. The severed heads of executed prisoners were displayed on the spikes of the impressive towers to deter would-be criminals.

outlawed cavaliers was very much a family affair: the men ordered to enforce the above-quoted commission included John Gordon of Park, James Gordon of Letterfourie and George Gordon of Beldornie, each of whom was closely related to at least one of the accused.

Even so, it had some effect. By 11 June 1635, seven of the Cabrach's 43 wanted men had been hunted down and killed, including Adam Gordon the Younger of Auchnacrie, whose severed head was set up on the Netherbow Port in Edinburgh. However, James Gordon of Letterfourie may have under-performed in his enforcement duty, or even refused to perform it, since he was called on the Privy Council carpet soon afterwards. Ross, 'one of the principal rebels and disobedient persons in the north', was captured, but was shortly after rescued with considerable violence by one William Gordon from Migvie, who returned him to Huntly's palace of Strathbogie where he was apparently in no further danger from royal justice. Alexander Leith remained on the loose, as did his second-in-command, another Adam Gordon, who was a brother of both the first laird of Park and the third laird of Glenbuchat. A whole quarter-century after we first met them, we should be struck by the Cabrach population's lopsidedly high social standing, its unusual geographic mobility, its sheer size, and its willingness to use extreme violence for a variety of purposes, both legal and illegal.

II
Nursery of the Royalist Cavalry

'Within the whilk hous . . . so robbed, spoilyed and plundered be the saids rebellis thair wes ane great aquavitie pott perteining to the supplicant, worth ane hundreth merks'

Scottish Parliament, *Act in Favour of James, Lord Coupar*, 1649

Whatever else they may have been, most of the Cabrach gang – like their original sponsor, Lord Huntly, who died of natural causes in 1636 – were Roman Catholics. This had only been mildly problematic when the Royal House of Stuart was able to enforce moderation and toleration in the running of Scotland's established Protestant Church; but when much of Scotland burst out into a frenzy of ultra-Protestant revolution at the end of the same decade, the Cabrach cavaliers and their wider webs of relations and criminal contacts rapidly reinvented themselves as preservers of the status quo. Meanwhile, their hereditary enemy, Archibald Campbell, 8th Earl of Argyll, who boasted 20,000 retainers at this time, placed himself at the head of the revolutionary Covenanters, who saw 'Popish' plotters under every bed. So the typical Cabrach swordsman, whatever his personal feelings about (or past conflicts with) the order-obsessed King Charles I, would have favoured the king's side almost as a matter of course.

Lesmoir Castle, a naturally strong, moated Norman manor, became a royal garrison: commanded not by its Gordon owner (though he was also a Royalist) but by the same John Leith of Harthill who had occupied the lands of Denscheill in Cabrach in the 'teens. The hills of Banffshire in general quickly became a key place of refuge for nearly anyone out of step with the authority of the Covenanting regime. The people of Strathbogie, as the town of Huntly was still known, began using Glenfiddich and Auchindoun as hiding places for their moveable goods; at least one Gordon lady who had been threatened by the revolutionaries fled to Lesmoir in 1643. Most spectacularly, two of Lord Huntly's sons raised a force of more than 200 Lowland cavalry – including a large number of fully armoured cuirassiers – that joined the otherwise Highland and Irish Royalist army led by the Marquess of Montrose. As in the clan battles of the previous century, the Gordon horsemen's contribution was frequently decisive. At the battles of Auldearn in Nairn in May 1645, Alford on Donside in July, and Kilsyth near Stirling in August – due in large measure to the Gordon horse's ability to outrun the fleeing enemy – the Royalists killed 7,500 Covenanters: a number more than twice as large as their own army's

The magnificent Huntly (Strathbogie) Castle, the ancestral seat of the Gordon Earls of Huntly.

highest strength at any given time. Though King Charles was ultimately doomed, this lightning campaign on his behalf ruined Scotland's revolutionary state both financially and militarily, and forced the scaling-back of Scottish military operations in support of the Roundheads down in England. And as the camaraderie of this amazing Royalist campaign knitted its members ever closer together, the Gordons' exposure to the Highland and Irish cultures – and therefore to whisky – was inevitable; one of the many things they stole from Covenanter civilians was a large whisky still 'worth 100 merks'[10]. Indeed, for the Cabrach and its people, the Civil War meant a 180-degree reversal of the peacetime situation in which Lowland manners and customs had been expected inevitably to triumph over Highland ones.

III
The Campbells Triumphant and the Coming of Smuggling

'[*By*] *secrett contrivance ... sundry persons ... did take all advantages of inciteing the people, not soe much against the* [*Excise tax*] *openly, as the persons* [*sent to collect it*]'

Thomas Tucker, *Report . . . upon the Settlement of the Revenues of the Excise and Customs in Scotland*, 1656

Not all of the Highland-isation of Cabrach society was benign, however. Old Huntly's son, the 2nd Marquess of Huntly, was estimated *before* the commencement of hostilities as being one million merks in debt (a sum equivalent to at least £8 million and as much as £285 million today, depending on how the money would have been used). The fact that this estimate was provided by his brother-in-law and great enemy Archibald Campbell, who became 1st Marquess of Argyll in 1641, reflects the latter's role in the 'predatory lending' that had placed the younger Huntly in this fix to begin with. However, Gordon of Lesmoir – the richest and most senior nobleman to be mixed up in the affairs of the Cabrach on a day-to-day basis – had also loaned his cousin Huntly 26,000 merks. Especially for the nobility, who as in medieval times still bore the financial brunt of recruiting and equipping the soldiers of both sides, war would prove an even more expensive business than peace. Not coincidentally, it is also in the early 1640s that smuggling originates.

First in England in 1643, and then in Scotland the following year, specifically for the purpose of financing revolutionary military activity in both countries,[11] excise taxes were levied on a wide range of commodities, including spirits. The onerous novelty of the tax, which was due at the time and point of manufacture rather than of import or export, was seen as mirroring the suspect novelty of these regimes more generally. This suspicion was particularly marked among the peoples of Britain's rural uplands and smaller port towns, who already tended to favour the Royalist cause. Their reaction was immediate and unanimous. 'Within months' of the imposition of the Scottish Excise in 1644,[12] according to historian and former excise officer S.W. Sillett, the nation 'was convulsed by smuggling operations of every kind. On the coast . . . companies were formed to operate ships in the illicit trade.' Over the whole country, only a fraction of the whisky manufactured was entered for duty. Virtually everybody joined in the smuggling activities.

From this moment, in other words, hitherto fairly diffuse popular objections to Puritanism, to violent political revolution and to the Campbells as a group of people slipped into smuggling as a hand slips into a glove.

Despite the revenue that accrued to the Gordons and other anti-Covenanting gentry by these methods, the military picture for the Royalists soon became dire. In 1646, the king gave himself up to the Covenanters' army, and Lord Montrose – having finally been defeated at Philiphaugh in the Borders – left for Norway. The Gordons' small army occupied the town of Banff throughout the winter of 1646–47 in the vain hope that the king would somehow manage to join them there; but he remained in the custody of the enemy. Disaster struck nearer to home in March 1647 when the Covenanters captured Lesmoir Castle, summarily executing 27 members of the garrison and burning the village of Lesmoir to the ground.[13] Patrick Leith of Harthill, presumably the heir of Lesmoir's Cabrach-dwelling commandant, was excommunicated from the Presbyterian Church due to his Royalist political stance in the same year.[14] However, the nadir of the Gordons' fortunes was yet to come: for 1649 saw the executions of the king in January, and of the 2nd Marquess of Huntly in March, at which Huntly's heir James, Viscount Aboyne – a veteran and undefeated cavalry commander at the age of 28 – is said to have died of grief. Aboyne's elder brother Lord Gordon had already been killed in the saddle at the Battle of Alford.

The House of Gordon's principled but un-shrewd refusal to accept the ever more popular Presbyterian religion – even the Protestant 2nd Marquess of Huntly was an Episcopalian – meant that their Gaelic but Presbyterian rivals, the Campbells, would now vanquish them all but completely in the political and economic spheres. Absurdly, this process would continue to accelerate even after many of the Gordons and Campbells found common cause, as Scots, against the English Republic's invasion and 11-year occupation of Scotland that began in the summer of 1650. The Marquess of Argyll's son, Archibald Campbell of Lorne, either became a Royalist at this point or successfully convinced the Royalist guerrilla army that he had done so. In practice, this involved him taking over the financial affairs of the Cabrach and providing its church with a resident Presbyterian minister, James Rosse – perhaps the first such person allowed to set foot in the barony in its history.[15] An initially successful Royalist guerrilla campaign, run partly from the Cabrach, petered out in 1654, possibly due to Lorne's treachery.

Then, quite unexpectedly, the tables turned again. Lorne was imprisoned for his Royalist or pseudo-Royalist military activities by the occupying army of the English Republic in 1657, but then maintained in custody for three more years after the 1660 Restoration of the Monarchy – probably through 'guilt by association' with his father Argyll, who was executed in 1661 for his leading role in the Scottish Revolution over the preceding quarter-century. Reverend Rosse

A mid-seventeenth-century description of the vessels used in distilling spirits.

and others who had been given land and positions in the Cabrach by the Campbells were expelled in 1662. The Gordon kindred then came home to the Cabrach to roost, accompanied for the first time by a large number of Stewarts,[16] and were allowed by the new king to establish a horse fair in Kirkton of Cabrach in 1669. The two leading members of the Gordon family, the 4th Marquess of Huntly and the 1st Earl of Aboyne, were both able to return to peaceable horse-trading: the former as the avid owner of a string of racehorses, one worth 100 guineas (up to £2.4 million at today's values), the latter as patron and chief beneficiary of the Cabrach horse fair. Both men were, according to the House of Gordon's leading historian, Barry Robertson, 'open to using violence and intimidation' in their business dealings.[17] And, just as in James VI's reign three-quarters of a century earlier, they hired Highland mercenaries and lesser Gordon lairds to do their dirty work. The particular laird/enforcers in question, as of 1680, included at least three grandsons of the same gentlemen who had filled the identical role from their base in the Cabrach in 1610: Gordon of Lesmoir, Gordon of Knockespock and Gordon of Cocklarachie.

This was very far indeed from being a complete restoration of pre-war Cabrach society, however. The advent during the war years of major commercial distilling – and of smuggling – had changed it forever. Lords Huntly and Aboyne, deeply dodgy though they might have been from the point of view of both the Kirk and the law, both became Excise Commissioners – at a time when it was being loudly complained of in the Scots Parliament 'that barley ... [is] the commodity which bears the greatest burden of the excise'.[18]

Overleaf.
Latterly a major fishing port, in earlier times Buckie Harbour played a key role in supporting the smuggling of illicit whisky.

IV
Resistance Continues: The Ferintosh Years

'Circumstances gave the Running Trade the Appearance of absolute Security . . . For twenty Years after the Union . . . the Use of home-made Spirits [was] almost universally laid aside'

Some Considerations on the Present State of Scotland, 1744

No firm date for the founding of the famous or infamous Ferintosh whisky distillery has ever been established, though most scholars assume it occurred around 1670. However, when the English Puritan occupation government divided Scotland into 21 districts for the purposes of excise collection on all types of domestically produced alcohol in January 1656, all of these districts were counties or cities – except 'Farintosh', which was exempted by name from the Elgin and Nairn district. This strongly implies that there was *already* a distillery on the Ferintosh estate in the Civil War period and, since this enterprise was not mentioned in 1626 when the estate was sold to the Forbeses by the Mackintoshes,[19] it could only have been founded by one of two people: Duncan Forbes MP, who was Provost of Inverness while Huntly was still Sheriff of Inverness-shire down to 1629, or else by Forbes's son John, who was Provost of Inverness for eight years in the 1640s and '50s.

Like so many of their own clan, and their great friends the Lords Argyll, the Forbeses of Culloden were staunch Calvinists and very much a thorn in the Huntly family's side during the sixteenth, seventeenth and eighteenth centuries.[20] As such, even before the Ferintosh Distillery was given its notorious de facto monopoly of legal whisky production on 22 July 1690 – when it was described in parliament as 'an ancient brewery of whisky' – the enterprise was associated with nearly everything that the House of Gordon had ever stood against: in culture (Highland and Gaelic[21]), religion (Presbyterian), faction (Campbell) and general political outlook (anti-Royalist).

The reason for the Ferintosh monopoly being granted, moreover, was nakedly political. King James VII and II, a Catholic, had been overthrown in a military coup by his Dutch Calvinist nephew/son-in-law, William of Orange, the previous year. Armed resistance by King James's supporters was not long in coming. They were known as Jacobites because James was referred to as 'Jacobus' on the nation's coinage and official documents. The Marquess of Huntly, who had become Duke of Gordon in 1684, held Edinburgh Castle for King James for several months and many of his kinsmen fought against the Williamites in the hills, to no avail. The burning down of the Ferintosh

Resistance Continues: The Ferintosh Years

All that remains of the historic Ferintosh Distillery.

Distillery was in fact one of the most notable successes in the first Jacobite Rising of 1689–92. The Jacobites were defeated repeatedly in the field over the next 54 years, while in Edinburgh the naturally pro-Williamite Campbells of Argyll came to dominate national politics completely, mixing 'naked ambition . . . with promoting economic and social modernization'.[22] Like his forefathers, Duncan Forbes of Culloden remained among the most loyal of the Campbells' political henchmen. During the century and more in which Forbes's Ferintosh dominated Scotland's domestic drinks trade, with a market share estimated at 50–65 per cent, the word 'Ferintosh' actually became a synonym for 'whisky' in general. Any loyal Gordon kinsman might easily have felt himself bound by honour and duty to avoid the stuff – and, if necessary, to procure alternatives to it, however and whenever he could.

In parallel to Jacobite military intrigue, the strategy for doing so quickly became highly international and grand in ambition and scale. By the time of the last Stuart monarch, Queen Anne (r. 1702–14), Scottish merchant skippers were considered the most active and cunning smugglers in the entire world – and if these smugglers were mostly fervent Jacobites, this merely reflected the outlook of the Scottish mercantile community as a whole.[23] At the very centre of this lucrative web of intrigue, we find Robert Gordon: a high-level smuggler based in Bordeaux, who was 'deeply immersed in Jacobite conspiracy'.[24] There were, in all, at least 33 Jacobite merchant houses in France and Belgium, 16 in

Scandinavia and 15 in Spain, employing thousands of individuals and heavily involved in the illegal shipment of brandy into Britain. Brandy was even used as ballast in ships running other illegal commodities, or as a 'pretext' for the clandestine shipment of Jacobite plotters' correspondence.[25] When the *Anne* of Inverness – her name suggestive of Stuart loyalism – ran aground off Newburgh, Aberdeenshire, in November 1728, laden with 'Dutch goods pretending to be bound for Norway', the Duchess of Gordon appeared. Invoking her hereditary feudal rights as a Vice-Admiral of the Coast of Scotland, she claimed 'the Burgundy and Champaign' from the wreck for her own use.[26]

Glasgow riots against the Malt Tax in 1725, which included the destruction of the magnificent town house of Daniel Campbell of Shawfield MP, led politician (and Ferintosh Distillery owner) Duncan Forbes to have a group of Glasgow city officials arrested for not taking a hard enough line with the rioters. A few years later, at the hanging of a smuggler in Edinburgh's Grassmarket, a pro-smuggling crowd assembled and the City Guard fired into it, killing six people and wounding several others. Amid his maniacal personal crusade against brandy smuggling, Forbes defended the city's actions, even though the captain of the guards was convicted of murder (and later lynched). It is quite clear that suppressed political feelings – whether for the exiled House of Stuart or against the 1707 Act of Union, or both – were being played out through the smuggling enterprise. A parliamentary act of 1736 prescribed the death penalty for smugglers who wounded officers, which paradoxically led to an increase in violence as the desperados now had even more reason to avoid capture. Unsurprisingly, given this background, the General Assembly of the Kirk felt compelled to condemn smuggling in 1719, 1736 and 1744. By the latter year, a contemporary wrote,

> The *Smuggler* was the Favourite. His prohibited or high Duty Goods were run ashore by the Boats of whatever Part of the coast he came near; when ashore, they were guarded by the Country from the Custom-house-officer; if seized, they were rescued; and if any Seizure was returned and tried, the *Juries* seldom failed to find for the Defendant. These Circumstances gave the *Running* Trade the Appearance of absolute Security; and have so *thoroughly* destroyed the Revenue, that the Customs are hardly able to pay the salaries of their own Officers ... For twenty Years after the Union [i.e. from 1707 to 1727] ... the Use of home-made Spirits [was] *almost universally* laid aside.[27]

The final defeat of Jacobitism in the field took place on Culloden Moor in 1746. But as many as nine years later the appointment of secret Jacobites to the excise

Resistance Continues: The Ferintosh Years

department – especially in Aberdeenshire – was 'common', despite the fact that Jacobites across Britain and Ireland 'condemned customs houses, excise officers, and the standing army as the tools of a corrupt and tyrannical ministry'.[28] It was even feared that 'many' persons in the revenue service might 'turn Jacobites, for fear they should be ruined' by their colleagues if they did not. An investigation into the matter of former officers of the Jacobite army penetrating the excise service was authorised by the Prime Minister in January 1754 but successfully obstructed by the Scottish Excise Board.[29] Certainly, a number of militarily active Cabrach Jacobites and their sons are known to have obtained, or regained, lucrative positions in the post-Culloden state or the administrative staff of the Duke of Gordon.[30] And despite the efforts of Duncan Forbes and others, foreign brandy – much of it having lined the pockets of former or current Jacobite Gordons living abroad – would remain Scotland's most-smuggled product from the 1710s to the 1770s.[31]

One leading historian has commented that 'lingering Jacobite sentiment' played a small part in the Cabrach's industrial-scale distilling of illicit whisky that began in the 1760s or '70s.[32] But, as we have seen, the true basis of the Cabrach smuggling phenomenon was much older than Jacobitism – and much angrier and more violent than the phrase 'lingering sentiment' could possibly convey.

Below.
A winter view of the Cabrach, with Auchindoun Castle.

Overleaf.
The Battle of Culloden, 16 April 1746.

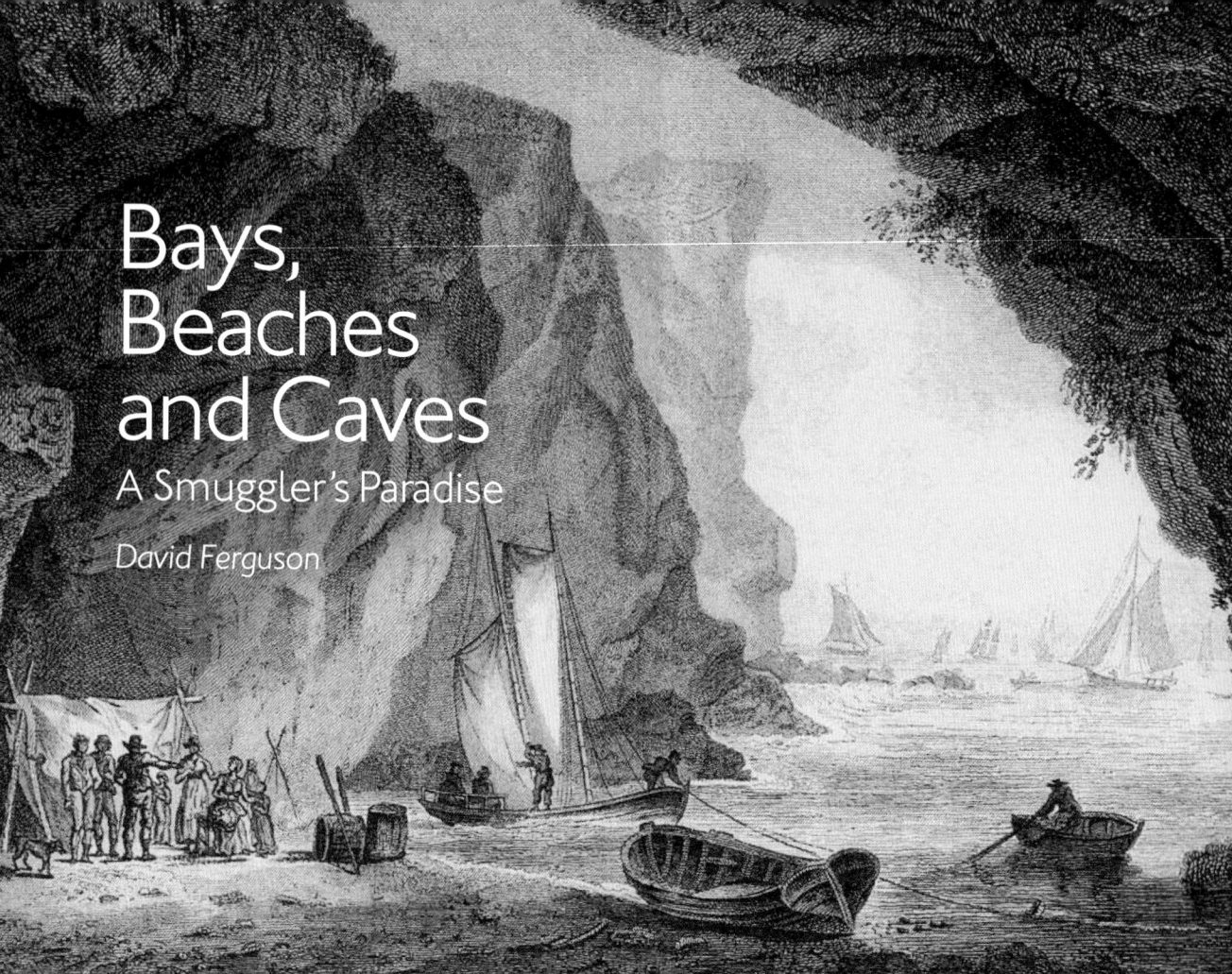

Bays, Beaches and Caves
A Smuggler's Paradise

David Ferguson

The 1707 Treaty of Union was something of a forced marriage. After Scotland's disastrous Darien colonial adventure, the country's finances were in a shambles.

The Union was also the catalyst for one of the largest acts of defiance against laws instigated by England, which were seen as oppressive and wholly unjust. With the Scottish currency worth a fraction of the English pound, new taxes and imposts based on the latter caused a mass disobedience by a population whose majority lived in grinding poverty. It is therefore perhaps not surprising that a significant portion of Scotland's economic activity in the eighteenth and early nineteenth centuries involved smuggling.

In addition to the massive quantity and variety of goods which were illegally shipped into the country at this time, locally produced illicit whisky was sold, or often traded for other smuggled goods – not least highly valued French brandy. A list of goods seized by the authorities in Aberdeen, dated November 1721, gives some idea of the huge variety of items being smuggled:

> 80 ankers containing 672 gallons brandy
> 5½ hogsheads and 11 ankers containing 446 gallons brandy
> 35 matts containing 3059 lbs leaf tobacco
> 10 small casks containing prunes
> 4 small casks containing raisins
> 2 small casks of sweet liquorice
> 2 hampers of earthenware
> 2 casks containing molasses
> 1 cask black pepper
> 32 firkins and 10 half firkins of soap
> 6 casks of anniseed
> 22 reams of writing paper
> 111 bars of Swedish iron

All levels of the population were involved; indeed, it was not unknown for some of the more flexible-minded members of the clergy to turn a blind eye, or to even have barrels of spirits hidden under their pulpits. To some extent, the whole of Scotland was directly or indirectly involved in smuggling.

While some of the illicit whisky distilled in the Highlands was 'exported' south using a network of old drove roads and tracks, the coast of the north-east of Scotland was a positive smuggler's paradise, with hundreds of bays, beaches and caves providing ideal sites where spirits could be shipped out, or traded for incoming smuggled goods, which would be brought ashore and concealed.

Occasionally the gaugers, the foot-soldiers of the customs and excise, would be forewarned of an impending smuggling operation and the resulting encounter could be lethal.

In the late eighteenth and early nineteenth centuries, the village of Collieston, sandwiched between Newburgh and Cruden Bay north of Aberdeen, became one of the main centres for the landing of smuggled goods. Writing in 1801, Collector Allardyce of Aberdeen Customs described Collieston as 'the principal haunt of the smugglers for landing goods', whose inhabitants were 'a turbulent riotous pilfering set'.

Collieston's most famous smuggler was Philip Kennedy, who earned his fame not through his exploits as a smuggler but because of his courageous defence of his illicit goods and his tragic death following a blow from a custom officer's cutlass in 1798. His grave in Slains Kirkyard can still be seen to this day.

One of the most ingenious smuggling operations in the north of Scotland was based at Troup Head, a massive sandstone edifice over 300 feet high, located between Pennan and Crovie on the Moray Firth. The headland contains a labyrinth of caves, some of which can only be reached from the sea. In addition, local charts show that the seabed shelves rapidly to the base of the cliffs, allowing smuggling vessels to moor relatively close inshore — making them less obvious to inquisitive eyes.

The first stage of this highly successful operation involved the transport of casks of distilled spirits on horseback from the remote glens of upland regions such as the Cabrach and Glenlivet, via a complex network of byways, to the coast. The casks could then be loaded into small boats and ferried out to the northernmost part of Troup Head and concealed from prying eyes, sometimes behind an old ship's canvas sails.

Once a shipment was ready, a message would be sent to the relevant parties and a ship would slip in at night and load the contraband by boat directly from the largest cave on Troup Head, known as the Needle's Eye.

Opposite.
The Needle's Eye, Troup Head. Smugglers at the mouth of the cave prepare to transport their goods to the waiting ships offshore. John Claude Nattes, 1799.

Left.
Crovie and Troup Head: Together with the neighbouring village of Pennan, Crovie was a major centre of smuggling activity on the Moray Firth.

Overleaf.
Smugglers by George Moreland, c.1793. This scene fulfilled the late eighteenth-century audience's appetite for romance and adventure.

V
A Logic of Its Own:
From Smuggling to Distilling, 1760 to 1790

'However unaccountable, in such a place, the want of inns and alehouses may be . . . the inconveniencies attending it [are not] felt by travellers, because of the hospitality of the people'

Rev. James Gordon, 'Parish of Cabrach', *Statistical Account of Scotland*, 1791–99

The 1760s were a time of vast political change for Scotland and Britain, seeing the accession of a pluralist monarch, the defeat of the Whigs at the ballot-box and the formal renunciation of support for the Jacobite cause by both Louis XV and the Pope. Suddenly, there were no 'red lines' that prevented former Jacobites, or current Roman Catholics, from supporting the government. Coincidentally, it was also at around the time of George III's accession that the immediate economic consequences of the 1707 Union, hitherto almost entirely negative from a Scottish point of view, began to fade. And far from continuing to dominate Scottish politics and society, the Campbells of Argyll retreated into the relative obscurity that they have enjoyed ever since. But for the Gordons, at home and abroad, smuggling's profitable combination of political resistance with organised crime would long outlive the political conditions that had given rise to it.

Part of this was mere habit – smuggling had been a way of life in the northeast of Scotland for perhaps six generations by the time George III came to the throne – and part was the industrial scale of the illegal distribution networks that the Jacobite era had spawned. Its personnel, horses, routes and places of concealment were simply too good to give up. New products, including tea, were adopted enthusiastically, and any commodity with a high value by weight would do, even things like ladies' whalebone combs. However, illicit whisky had a crucial advantage. Because it was a domestic product, the distributors – hitherto reliant on at least two layers of accomplices, merchant skippers and foreign producers – could now rely on just one, the distillers, or even fill this role themselves. Indeed, the Cabrach's illicit-whisky industry that emerged during these three decades was remarkable for what the economists call 'vertical integration': with local people providing the barley, distilling sites and expertise, distillery guards, horses, horse-convoy guards – everything, in short, with the possible exception of retail selling in the towns and cities. By the end of this period, in fact, the Cabrach smuggling networks' need for labour had outstripped the local population's ability to supply it and outlaw types moved into the Cabrach from all over the kingdom.

A Logic of Its Own: From Smuggling to Distilling, 1760–1790

Reekimlane in the Cabrach has been a Gordon residence from the mid sixteenth century to the present day. In common with occupants of many other farms and crofts in the area, the Gordons of Reekimlane were actively involved in illicit distilling and smuggling. While serving no obvious agricultural purpose, the curious range of metre-high ramps attached to the building adjoining the house would have been ideal for loading and unloading malt and other goods in support of the Gordons of Reekaimlane's involvement in illicit distilling and smuggling operations.

The remains of an early kiln at Reekimlane, which has been the subject of a recent archaeological survey. A kiln of this type, along with the nearby abundance of fresh water, would have been crucial in enabling the operations necessary for the distilling of illicit whisky.

In the 1770s – the decade during which domestic illicit distilling suddenly replaced importation of foreign spirits as the main concern of Britain's revenue authorities – the Gordon rank and file were as much in control of the Cabrach as they had been a century and a half earlier. Twelve married Gordon men, two of them with Gordon wives, inhabited houses in Ardwell (later the Grouse Inn), Bank, Bracklach, Craigencat, Gauch, Hillock of Echt, Kirktown, Oldtown, Tornachelt and Whitehillock. One of the six houses in Largue, Cabrach, was given the name 'Letterfury' around this time: apparently as an homage (or perhaps parodic reference) to yet another family of Jacobite Gordon lairds who, like the Gordons of Beldornie, had shipped out and become wildly successful in the international drinks trade.[33] Tellingly, there were no ale-houses in the Cabrach at this date, but travellers through the parish did not find this inconvenient, due to the 'hospitality of the people'.[34]

In 1783, the last year of the ruinous American War of Independence, half of the British government's total annual revenue of £13 million came from excise duties; but it was calculated that the £6.5 million the excise department actually collected was just one-third of what was owed to it. In other words, if a way could be found to end the evasion of excise completely, the total income of the British state would exactly double. The Ferintosh Distillery paid a purely token annual duty of less than £23, fixed since the seventeenth century. Unsurprisingly, it was one of the first victims of ham-fisted and rather desperate governmental efforts to reform the collection of revenue. Yet, seven years after it first made domestic whisky-smuggling an enforcement priority,[35] the British government believed that it had successfully detected only 5 per cent of the estimated 21,000 illicit stills operating in the Highlands (which, for this purpose, now included the Cabrach).[36] Moreover, most or perhaps all of the excise officers operating in Banffshire in 1782 were permanently attached to a particular individual distiller who had taken out a licence; and there would be no centrally controlled roving enforcement against *unlicensed* stills for another 20 years.[37] By the mid-1790s, according to Cabrach's minister, the Reverend James Gordon, distilling – none of it licensed – consumed his parish's entire surplus of 200 bolls of barley, about 1,200 bushels or 12.5 tons.[38] If the reverend gentleman disapproved, however, he kept any such thoughts strictly to himself. A whisky free-for-all had begun; the Cabrach's 140-year-old smuggling network was now poised on the brink of its greatest success.

VI
After the Ferintosh: Cabrach Smuggling's Golden Age

*'Lieut. Randall RN . . . patrolling near the toll of Tyrebagger,
seized three carts and horses bringing eleven and a half ankers of whisky
into town from the Cabrach, under the protection of seven men, mostly
known as notorious smugglers'*

Caledonian Mercury newspaper, 24 May 1823

By the end of the eighteenth century, smugglers were travelling in large bands throughout the country, often in 'pony trains', with each horse typically carrying two nine-gallon barrels called ankers. Whisky was also hidden in the knapsacks of men impersonating soldiers (and 'even in some cases preceded by pipers'), inside the digestive tracts of dead but unplucked geese, in coffins and hearses, and even in sheet-iron 'belly canteens', made to simulate a pregnancy and holding two gallons.[39] Officials of the excise repeatedly pleaded for a large force of dragoons – heavy cavalry – as the only type of troops likely to defeat a typical smuggling gang in a stand-up fight. Indeed, sending unmounted troops against the fleet-footed smugglers was usually inconclusive, though the Cabrach men

The streets of Old Aberdeen.

achieved some notable tactical successes. On one occasion, Donald McKenzie, an excise officer based in Elgin, met up with ten marines in Dufftown, expressly 'to make search in Cabrach' for whisky and stills. On arrival, their way was blocked by 20 local men – also armed with the latest military weapons – who showered the troops with filthy expletives as well as three musket volleys. McKenzie was shot through the body and in the face but lived to give evidence against the two smugglers, James Gordon and William Gordon, who were taken prisoner. Both natives of the Cabrach, they pleaded guilty in the High Court of Justiciary to 'discharging loaded fire-arms, with intent to murder, or to do grievous bodily injury ... and more especially ... with intent to obstruct officers of the revenue in the discharge of their duty'.[40] They were sentenced to transportation for life, perhaps going on to enrich the criminal underworld of early Australia. But, typically, their 18 paramilitary confederates in the Cabrach escaped identification, let alone punishment.

Another bloody battle occurred on the streets of Old Aberdeen in the summer of 1820, between the excisemen and '15 or 16 Men ... from the Parish of Cabrach', armed with cudgels, firearms and stones. In addition to his weapons, each smuggler carried an anker of whisky, part of a hoard that had been concealed in the northern Aberdeen suburbs. It had been brought down from the Cabrach in six horse-drawn carts, which were then concealed at Middleton's Stables, North Street, and McHardy's Stables in Harriet Street. It seems fairly unlikely that the stables' owners were unaware of what the smugglers were up to. As usual, the Cabrach men got the better of the encounter: all but two of the excisemen were wounded, and all but one of the smugglers escaped.[41]

Some battles of this type received a great deal of publicity. In the same year, the Duke of Gordon famously delivered a speech in the House of Lords in which he pledged to cooperate with the excise on his lands. Reading between the lines, it is easy enough to interpret the Duke's comments as evidence that he had *not* been cooperating with the authorities up to that point. As Sillett explains,

> successful smuggling on a large scale had the immediate effect of raising the price of barley, which in turn, afforded the proprietors ... increased rents for inferior lands; frequently as much as three times their true value ...The illicit distiller, tenant and landlord were thus entirely interdependent[.]

Yet, the Duke's speech was no smokescreen; steps were taken. On the Gordon estates, a contemporary recalled, the smugglers 'had to be rooted out'. Nevertheless, His Grace

After the Ferintosh: Cabrach Smuggling's Golden Age

handled the business with great delicacy. He pensioned some, gave others better crofts and houses, and, in short, managed matters so adroitly that no complaint or grievance was heard in regard to the changes he adopted.[42]

In 1825, the Duke even paid more than £68 in legal fees (about £52,000 today) to defend Charles Stewart, his tenant in Haddoch, Cabrach, against a serious smuggling charge in the Court of Exchequer. Despite this somewhat astonishing intervention, Stewart was found guilty.[43]

It is a well-polished Scottish myth that illicit northern whisky was conveyed due south to the Central Belt, or even directly into England, exclusively by land. In fact, almost all of the very, very large quantities of whisky made in the Cabrach and adjacent areas was moved by land northward and eastward: to the ports of Inverness, Cullen, Banff, Portsoy, Rosehearty, Fraserburgh and (especially) Aberdeen. Much of this untaxed spirit was consumed directly by the people of these towns, while the surplus was exported by sea – not always to England. The firm of Christie & Mitchell, who advertised 'anckers' in the

The harbour at Doune (now Macduff) near Banff played a key role in supporting smuggling activity along the Moray Firth. Joseph McIntyre, 1876.

Aberdeen newspapers in the early nineteenth century, was in fact a prolific smuggling syndicate.[44] Richard Smith, grocer at 86 Broad Street, advertised 'Cabrach and Glenlivat WHISKY' alongside coffee, sugar and London porter in the *Aberdeen Journal*. His competitors Charles Fyfe & Co. proclaimed their stock of whisky 'equal to the best Smuggled'; they later claimed to be selling 'very fine' Cabrach whisky to other dealers, 'at the Distillers' prices'. In the same era, William Clark's shop at 8 King Street, Aberdeen, sold 'Fine Malt Whisky' for 8s 6d a gallon, but Cabrach whisky for 10s 6d a gallon – a 24 per cent premium.[45] In the city of Aberdeen, at least, Cabrach whisky was considered both essentially similar to, and just as good as, Glenlivet whisky throughout the 1820s and 1830s – that is to say, for many years after King George IV's first alleged patronage of smuggled Glenlivet made it the more famous of the two in England.

Demand was enormous. In 1823, the *Caledonian Mercury* reported that, even as the UK's new Coastguard service was on the verge of stamping out *foreign* smuggling, domestic smugglers

> carry on their trade of 'Mountain Dew' in the most daring manner . . . On Thursday morning last . . . a party belonging to that zealous officer, Lieut. Randall R.N. from the Bridge of Don, patrolling near the toll of Tyrebagger, seized three carts and horses bringing eleven and a half ankers of whisky into town from the Cabrach, under the protection of seven men, mostly known as notorious smugglers.[46]

Just one hour earlier, another inbound illicit whisky shipment of about the same size had been seized a mile south-west of the Aberdeen Bridge of Dee. Clearly, despite the Duke of Gordon's efforts to eradicate it on his estates in general, smuggling continued to thrive in one particular spot: in 1823, parliament heard that in the Cabrach smuggling remained the 'whole trade and occupation of the people'.[47] Nor was this mere political hyperbole. In an 1824 incident that was *not* reported in the newspapers, excisemen on the northern outskirts of Aberdeen captured 'two notorious delinquents' from Powneed, Cabrach, with eight horses, six carts and 190 gallons of whisky. The arrested men had 'respectable farms' and 'good circumstances' in the Cabrach, 'having accumulated wealth from smuggling alone, for a number of years'.[48]

Comfort, however, placed no check on the smugglers' boldness. Alexander Gordon, an exceptionally notorious smuggler born in Largue, Cabrach, in 1798 or 1799, was as likely as not a direct descendant of Lord Huntly's enforcers, the lairds of Cocklarachie, millionaires in modern terms, who had occupied the same site in the seventeenth century.[49] One morning in early April 1822, as the ash trees were just coming into bud, Lt Henry Randall of the Bridge of Don

After the Ferintosh: Cabrach Smuggling's Golden Age

Distilling apparatus, from *The Art of Distillation*, 1651.

Coastguard Station, along with boatmen James Miles and John Rouse, hid near the wooden bridge over the River Don on the Grandholm estate 'for the purpose of intercepting smuggled Goods'. They soon spied 20 men, including Alexander Gordon, 'conveying a quantity of smuggled whisky across'. At considerable risk to their lives, the revenue men revealed themselves, approached the gang and boldly took possession of three and a half ankers by placing their hands on them and uttering the legally required words, 'We seize these spirits, and likewise the casks and vessels containing the same, for the proper use of His Majesty.' These barrels were left in the care of Rouse, while Miles and the lieutenant gave chase to the smugglers, who were fleeing in various directions through the ash and beech trees.[50]

But some of them only appeared to be fleeing. Alexander Gordon doubled back through the undergrowth, surprised the unfortunate Rouse and threw him to the ground, bludgeoning him on the head, arms and back with the butt of a pistol. Randall and Miles, alerted by Rouse's screams, returned to where they had left him. But it was too late: Gordon had robbed Rouse of his own pistol and cutlass, as well as one of the four seized barrels of whisky.[51] He was long gone, but would not be long in reappearing.

Three months later, no doubt acting on a tip-off from an informant, Robert Armstrong and Andrew Ritchie of the Peterhead Coastguard Station stood watch 'on the rising ground . . . commonly called the Heading Hill or Castle Hill of Aberdeen'. The tip was accurate enough: Alexander Gordon and two accomplices duly appeared, armed with bludgeons and rolling an anker of illicit Cabrach whisky through the middle of town in broad daylight. Unfortunately for Armstrong and Ritchie, they were overpowered by the three smugglers and severely beaten.[52]

Alexander Gordon was briefly captured that November but released after making a sworn statement to a justice of the peace.[53] The following year, however – amid widespread feeling that the JPs had been dealing too leniently with smugglers for many years – Gordon was hauled up in front of the High Court of Justiciary to answer for various felonies. Asked if he had been 'employed in conveying spirits to Aberdeen', he refused to give any answer. He admitted being at Grandholm on the date Boatman Rouse was assaulted but denied having seen any spirits seized, or anything unusual, and further claimed he was delivering a letter to the manager of a foundry near Grandholm regarding the purchase of a threshing machine. However, he could not 'describe the situation of the foundry or the owners thereof, or [give] the name of the person to whom [the] said letter was addressed'.[54] The trial lasted several hours and the judge instructed the jury that the case 'appeared to warrant a verdict of guilty'. Nevertheless, the jury returned a unanimous verdict of 'Not Proven'.[55] It is not certain that this Alexander Gordon was the same person who was later accused of attacking officers of the revenue at Perth in 1826, and again in 1828, and of 'assault by cutting or stabbing' in 1834.[56] But very intriguingly, from the point of view of the history of the later licit whisky industry, the baptism of the daughter of Alexander Gordon, the smuggler, was witnessed by his cousin, John Gordon from Reekimlane, Cabrach. This John's son, Charles Gordon, would grow up to marry the daughter of Major William Grant, founding proprietor of William Grant & Sons (himself a descendant of James Gordon, first laird of Lesmoir), and beget the future generations of the family that own the company to this day. And Janet, the smuggler's daughter, spent much of her long life as Reekimlane's housekeeper.

Banff
The Smuggler's Royal Burgh

Jay Wilson

As the crow flies north out of the hills of the Cabrach and Glenlivet, the nearest ports on the Moray Firth are Buckie and Banff. While Buckie offered a shorter, more direct route for the long strings of pack ponies laden heavily with illicit whisky, the Royal Burgh of Banff offered other advantages, foremost amongst these a coalition of duplicitous merchants and local lairds with their fleets safely anchored behind the town's vast shingle bar at the mouth of the River Deveron.

As Francis Wilkins writes in *The Smuggling Story of the Northern Shores*: 'Smugglers appear to have acted at will [in Banff] while the customs and other revenue officers struggled to undertake their duties with any degree of success.'

Circumnavigating officialdom to this degree would have been impossible to achieve without widespread community complicity, supported by the town's local mafia-style establishment. This extraordinary combination of factors enabled Banff to turn its remoteness into an advantage and in so doing become a law unto itself in the business of smuggling.

Early in 1780, whisky riots highlighted the strength of the town's involvement in the illicit trade. At this time, the Aberdeen tax collector admitted he had 'no good opinion of the procurator fiscal for Banffshire, [where there was] little chance of apprehending smugglers from any procedure of the Sheriff of Banff' (Wilkins, *The Smuggling Story*). The smugglers' spies swarmed the town and their lookouts covered the shires of both Banff and Moray, thereby further perverting the course of justice.

Duplicity appears to have come naturally to the smuggler merchants of Banff, who operated legitimate businesses in tandem with their illegal activities. For more than half a century, between 1785 and 1836, the town's business interests were championed by successive provosts (as mayors in Scotland are still known) who were members of the Robinson family. William Cramond in *The Annals of Banff* illustrates a curious example of their duplicity, which is provided by the actions of Provost George Robinson and his son, who both issued petitions to the Convention of Royal Burghs and prayed on behalf of their contemporaries 'for a

Above.
The bridge over the River Deveron, leading to Banff, with the Moray Firth in the distance.

Opposite.
George Robinson, Provost of Banff, 1784–1827.

customs house nearer than Aberdeen'. However, the information the burgh provided to John Forbes, Collector of Taxes in Aberdeen, stated that foreign trade amounted to 'next to nothing' and that coastal trade in the area comprised mainly fishing. It was also relayed that for the 18-month period between January 1785 and June 1786 the number of ankers (of whisky) leaving Fraserburgh, Doune (now called Macduff), Banff and Portsoy totalled a mere 142, while duty paid on alcohol was only from vessels 'forcibly carried in' by revenue ships. Therefore, and perhaps unsurprisingly, it was argued that the relative absence of declared trading on the Moray coast did not warrant a customs house.

As noted in James Findlay's *Wolfe in Scotland*, it often seemed to both outsiders and visitors that Banff's 'interests were not devoted to the neighbouring lands but were directed to shipping, and that smuggling was rife'. This was not altogether accurate, as lowland Banffshire harvested high-quality barley that commanded a premium price as whisky's chief raw material. The Parish of King Edward reported, in 1794, that its 'small [illicit] whisky stills afforded a good market for barley and supply us with good whisky of a quality greatly superior to what we have from the large [legitimate] stills in the southern districts' (*The Book of Banff*, Banff Preservation Society).

Wilkins describes how, over time, Banff earned a reputation for its 'barefaced practice' of smuggling. Excisemen frequently requested military assistance in their efforts to suppress it. One of them, David Cooper, became a victim of this brazen behaviour on 21 October 1732, when he was 'attacked and seized upon the High Street' by a gang of men pretending to be the Town Guard. In addition to preventing him from doing his duty as officer of the excise, they detained him in the tolbooth 'for some time'. Cramond, who recorded this incident in *The Annals of Banff*, does not enlighten us as to what was going on in town at the time, but one can surmise something was up, as the magistrates later found that the 'alleged' imprisonment was 'quite groundless'.

A major advantage of Banff to its smuggler merchants was the shingle bar, along its shoreline, which enabled the easy on- and off-loading of cargo directly onto the private wharves of the fine Georgian houses they had built, strung out along the street known as High Shore. Despite the lack of declared trade, it can be no coincidence that Banff's legacy of fine-built heritage sprang up in the heyday of illicit distilling and smuggling.

By the time the illicit trade was waning, Banff's smuggler merchants were beginning to carve out an image of respectability for themselves. James McKilligan (Provost 1831–33) established his distillery on the banks of the River Deveron, at the Mill of Banff, where he distilled and traded whisky without fear of the attention of the authorities.

Smuggling in Banff was not restricted to whisky. Any cargo on which taxes might be levied was fair game for the burgh's smuggler merchants and obviously the rewards outweighed the risks. It was in everyone's interest to be involved in a well-crafted operation. Although the smugglers carried all the risk, it was possible for everyone to gain. The tidesmen, first on the scene, claimed salvage rights. The military, called in by the tidesmen, were paid for securing the cargo. The Revenue Office, in the end, still received the duty. This kind of operation is perfectly illustrated in the case of the *Jean*, of Findhorn.

Early in November 1780, she was running a cargo into Banff for a Forres merchant. A vicious storm blew up and beached her on the shingle bar. Three excise officers from Doune — Robert Henry, Thomas Milne and James McNure — were first on the scene and secured it with military aid. Salvage value alone placed on the cargo of 'seventy one boxes, forty three casks of tea and two sets of china' was £2,057. This included neither the damaged casks of tea valued at £1,400 and burned, nor the cargo which was smuggled ashore before the storm hit. Notwithstanding all of this, the smuggler merchant even got his ship back by

paying a bond of £52 to the Revenue Office, as it saved them the trouble of disposing of it.

In the autumn of 1765, while in Paris, Lord Fife himself dabbled in a spot of illicit trading. As described in Alistair and Henrietta Tayler's *Lord Fife and his Factor*, he sought advice on how to ship wine, French furnishings, damask, tapestries and glassware while keeping its shipping method secret from Baillie Hay in Banff, who 'would be very pleased if our little Cargo was seased' before it arrived at Duff House. He also complained openly in a letter to William Rose, his factor, that 'smuggling my things home has cost me a great deal of expense'. Transporting them in this manner, however, cost him a great deal less than legitimate means.

The key to success in Banff's business of smuggling appears to have been contacts, specifically family connections. Repeatedly, revenue officers were implicated in the burgh's inability to suppress the trade. According to Wilkins in *The Smuggling Story*, Robert McGilligan, tidesman at Gardenstown, was removed from his duties in 1765 by order of the Board of Customs due to his 'inactivities and [family] connections' in the area. But not everyone was caught out. One of the most prosperous Banff merchants of this time was James Duff, cousin to the 1st Earl of Fife. He lived in the town's Low Street and traded to a 'pretty considerable extent' in the major Scottish cities and ports of the south and west. From these trading voyages, he made 'such dispatch as was really incredible' (William Baird, *Genealogical Memoirs of the Duffs*). Coincidentally perhaps, his daughter Margaret was married twice, both times to Supervisors of Excise.

Time was running out for the burgh's smugglers. In 1825, an extension of the powers of Justices of Peace in the execution and administration of the revenue laws was granted. This effectively led to the two rooms allocated to debtors at Banff's prison becoming 'excessively crowded'; in that year, writes Cramond in *The Annals of Banff*, they held an average of 'above 20 [excise prisoners] while the whole number of debtors during that period had been only 4'.

Opposite.
Early eighteenth-century map of Banff.

Below.
It is no coincidence Banff's fine-built heritage sprang up in the heyday of illicit distilling and smuggling.

VII
Passing into History?

'[A] fresh generation of smugglers has been trained, and time, hard work, and money will be required to suppress the evil'

Ian MacDonald, *Smuggling in the Highlands*, 1914

By the early 1830s, when Corgarff Castle's 58-man anti-smuggling garrison was reassigned to less quiet places, nearly everyone supposed that the smuggling era was a thing of the past. Cabrach's census returns for 1841 and 1851 suggest otherwise: with microscopic 'farms' employing dozens of men and generating large, inexplicable sums of cash.

Alexander Gordon in Auchmair, Cabrach, was described in the 1851 census as a farmer of four acres employing two labourers, supporting a family of four and entertaining a visitor, Robert Milne from Forfarshire, 'Hawker of Cloth'. Given that rates of male wages in the Cabrach were 2s a week or more, Auchmair was apparently generating not merely 150–200 per cent of the maximum theoretical food supply for a farm of its size – at the height of the Highland Potato Famine! – but an additional £11 sterling per year in cash. Only a profitable, undeclared business could explain this cash flow, or indeed why the workmen who received some share of it were needed at Auchmair in the first place.

When Jean Gordon from the Cabrach farm known as Bank was tried for large-scale sheep-rustling in 1841, her defence attorney argued – successfully – that 'notwithstanding the great amount of civilization and education now prevalent', the people of the Cabrach still had 'very loose notions' of what was legal or illegal.[57] It also helped that – apart from lone excisemen living and working full-time at a small handful of licensed distilleries – there were no fixed excise premises nearer to the Cabrach than Huntly, a distance of 18 miles by road. It would thus have taken any given riding officer a whole day to get to the Cabrach and home again, quite apart from any inspecting he tried to do while he was there. The typical long-distance speed of a man on a horse being 4 mph, and given a typical 12-hour working day, a riding officer from Huntly would either have had to spend less than three hours inspecting the whole of the Cabrach or risk his neck by staying in the district overnight. This problem alone would serve to explain why intervention in the Cabrach was so rare and prosecutions so few; and why most of the Cabrach men arrested for smuggling in the previous half-century were caught not in their native hills but on the city streets of Aberdeen.

Passing into History?

Unsurprisingly, given their durable basis in family relationships, links between the Cabrach and southern Europe's drinks trade also persisted well into the nineteenth century – long after the Jacobite politics that gave rise to these networks had become a mere historical curiosity. For instance, John David Gordon, the future 12th laird of Beldornie, married Maria del Carmen Beigbeider of Jerez de la Frontera, Spain, in 1805. He thereafter 'lived at that place and devoted his attention to the wine business' – the English word 'sherry' is a corrupt version of 'Jerez' – but continued diligently to oversee his Scottish estates by post.[58] His eldest son married Rosa Elena Prendergast of Cadiz, a second cousin. Though this couple had no surviving children, the title to Beldornie then passed to another Scottish-resident Gordon laird of the same hybrid Spanish stock and succeeding generations continued to marry their Spanish cousins.[59] We should not be surprised that when there was a marked revival of illicit distilling in the late Victorian era the Beldornie estate was very much at its centre. One of the most prolific and successful illicit distillers of this period was James 'Goshen' Smith, Beldornie's gamekeeper and 'the most cunning chemist in Strathbogie'. A gentleman who had sampled Goshen's whisky whilst on holiday at Beldornie inadvertently led to the distiller's downfall by praising the quality of the brew to a dinner-party companion in London,

Left.
Victorian photograph of the original bridge at Glen Grant Distillery on Speyside.

Right.
Recently restored rustic bridge and dramming hut at Glen Grant, which, from the late nineteenth century to the present day, acknowledges and celebrates what was an early illicit distilling site.

who turned out to be a high-ranking excise official! This occurred in early 1888 and led to a careful search of every inhabited place between Stoniley, the croft where Goshen himself lived, and the Grouse Inn. Goshen was tried in Keith in April 1888, found guilty and fined £10.[60] 'Since 1880,' a different exciseman wrote in 1914, 'a fresh generation of smugglers has been trained, and time, hard work, and money will be required to suppress the evil. Indeed, in some places it will only die out with the men.'[61] Statistics seem to bear this out: the overall number of still-seizures nationally fell from 692 in 1834 to 177 ten years later, then to 73 in 1854, 19 in 1864 and just six in 1874. A decade later, however, this number nearly quadrupled to 22. As always, the dice of the legal system seemed loaded in the culprits' favour. Robert McIntosh, merchant in Cabrach, was found guilty of selling whisky without a licence in the summer of 1890 but appealed on the grounds that one of the Huntly JPs who had convicted him was also a revenue officer. He was re-tried, without the officer being present, but appealed again, on the common-law grounds that a person cannot be tried twice for the same offence![62]

In the absence of any town per se or resident nobleman, the schoolmaster of Cabrach in the nineteenth century was in some respects its 'squire'. Schoolmasters fed the poor, built bridges and shielded the distillers as best they could: William Ronald with the pen and Thomas Robertson, apparently, with a gun. Excisemen's lore suggests that Robertson escaped prosecution for the shooting to death of an officer in the 1880s and we know that he kept his post as schoolmaster until his death in 1909. One rather more comical Cabrach escapade in Edwardian times involved an illicit still being hidden in a peat hag,[63] and the *Aberdeen Journal* declared somewhat hyperbolically in 1906 that whisky smuggling was 'beginning again to assume formidable proportions'.[64] The smuggler, the same article went on to explain,

> instead of the romantic creature depicted in literature, is usually a very low type of Highlander, much addicted to drinking, laziness, and lying. In fact he bears a strong resemblance to the poacher found in all parts of Scotland. He may pass as a dyker, fencer, or stonebreaker, but he has no fixed trade... At intervals he disappears – perhaps for days – during which he is likely in his 'bothy' or dissipating with his fraternity.

Drastic increases in taxation that were required to support the war effort from 1914 to 1918 undoubtedly led to further evasion and various allusions to this were made in the long, rambling and very funny poem *Tibby Tamson o' the Buck*, published by John Mitchell in support of the Gordon Highlanders' Prisoners of War Fund in 1917. The eponymous Cabrach heroine is supportive of the war but critical of how it is being handled by Lloyd George's government:

Opposite.
A nineteenth-century tableau of smuggling in the Highlands, which champions the capture and destruction of an illicit still.

SMUGGLING IN THE HIGHLANDS—THE CAPTURE OF AN ILLICIT WHISKY STILL.

> They've commandeert the tatties, an' they've commandeert the hay,
> They've commandeert the corn an' meal, forbyes the neeps and strae,
> They've commandeert the fusky that keeps oot the caul an' wet
> If they commandeert some common-sense, we'd get tae Berlin yet.

Needless to say, like four centuries of her forefathers and foremothers, Tibby keeps 'a knaggie in the press' from which she offers her frequent visitors 'a skirp o' barley-bree' – though she herself 'dinna haud wi' drink'!

James McIntosh, proprietor of the Gordon Arms Hotel in Keith, was caught distilling without licence in a secret cellar of the hotel with an accomplice named James Carter; the pair was fined £200 on 8 January 1934.[65] Just two months later, A.R. Birnie's Scots comedy play *Mountain Dew*, characterised by its 'many amusing incidents' from 'the days of illicit distilling and smuggling', was staged on Deeside to great popular and critical acclaim.[66] Keith hotel case notwithstanding, the playwright was probably not far wrong in assigning his story to a bygone age. By this time, prison terms were more frequently handed out instead of or in addition to fines, which were themselves much stiffer in real terms than they had ever been before. To cite an extreme example, John Sutherland – 'refreshment house keeper' – was fined £75 in lieu of six months' imprisonment in the spring of 1928, for 'selling two bottles of beer at a dance . . . by the hands of a friend'.[67] Perhaps unsurprisingly, in the face of such draconian punishments, fewer than a dozen crimes of illicit distilling were reported by the *Aberdeen Journal* in the whole of the 1920s – and none occurred in the north-east of Scotland (one involved 'two crofters' in Ross-shire, one a baker in West Dunbartonshire, and one a 'Russian subject' making vodka in Stepney, East London).[68] Such cases were newsworthy UK-wide, due to their rarity and the steepness of the fines levied.

Rationing led to another minor resurgence in the 1940s, mostly in urban areas,[69] but one old hand who had been active in the trade on Highland Deeside in the late 1870s declared that '[n]owadays there is no illicit distilling . . . They don't know how'.[70] Nevertheless, after spending considerable time in the Cabrach as an excise officer, S.W. Sillett felt in 1965 that illicit whisky distilling might still be going on there.[71] Perhaps we will never know for certain when, or if, it came to an end. But it is now absolutely clear that the old stereotype of Scottish illicit distilling as a marginal, almost solitary activity that made no one rich is – at least in the case of the north-east – absurd.[72] The stereotype view also holds that whisky made in the Highlands was invariably bought wholesale at the point of manufacture by 'regularly trained smugglers' who were 'strangers from outside the district of manufacture . . . generally Irishmen or Lowlanders',[73] and conveyed – always by land – directly to the cities of the Central Belt or across the border into England. However, the present case study of the north-

Passing into History?

Whisky smugglers secretly making plans, mid-eighteenth century.

east of Scotland has exploded all elements of this view, revealing that highly organised *local* gangs (often with roots in the area going back to the seventeenth century or further) might control integrated networks of production and distribution, aimed at northern port towns, presumably with a view to shipment abroad; that the controllers of such networks *did* become rich from them in many cases; and that if Edinburgh, Glasgow and England formed any part of the eventual retail market for north-eastern whisky, it was moved there by ship. Nor would there have been anything to prevent local sub-distribution by rowboat, as is known to have occurred in eighteenth-century Ireland.[74] 'The Cabrach' was made, moved and sold on an industrial scale; and this was just one part of a multi-generational criminal enterprise, deeply rooted in politics, and involving the entire community.

Scotland's Lost Distilleries

Brian Townsend

For every distillery operating in Scotland today, countless others, legal and illegal, have vanished over the years. From the seventeenth to the nineteenth centuries, thousands of tiny distilleries were established, flourished and waned. For every one that was legal and registered, many more were not. As such, the precise number is not known.

Illegal distilling was spurred on by taxation, in the form of Excise Duty, which was first introduced in the 1640s. After the union of the Scottish and English parliaments in 1707, the department of customs and excise was created to collect the tax, using the dreaded excisemen or gaugers — a key aspect of whose work involved hunting down illicit distillers and smugglers. During the following years parliament increased taxes on distilling — thereby driving many legal distillers either to ruin or to become illegal. In addition to which chronic shortages of barley, caused by the bad harvests of the 1790s, riots and widespread public unrest, and the Napoleonic Wars, which created further shortages and havoc, resulted in scores of distilleries in Scotland and Ireland closing down.

Salvation came in the form of two government acts that, in hindsight, could be said to have spawned Scotland's modern whisky industry. The first was the 1823 Excise Act, which halved spirit duty, set a 40-gallon-minimum still size (too big to be easily hidden or for one man to carry on his shoulders) and an affordable £10 licence fee —

which led to dozens of illegal distillers turning legit. This was followed in 1846 by the repeal of the import-stifling Corn Laws, which enabled distillers to obtain at low cost barley, wheat and maize — the new starch-rich grain from North America — in world markets. Add to this the effect of the Industrial Revolution, the mushroom growth of railways and an expanding customer base, and all the building blocks were in place for the beginning of the Scotch whisky industry to begin its 75-year-long first Golden Age.

Then the dark times began: a high-profile blender, Pattisons of Leith, went bust, badly denting industry finances and confidence. Under pressure from the temperance movement, Chancellor David Lloyd George nearly doubled the Spirit Duty in 1909. The coming of the First World War closed down almost all of Scotland's malt distilleries, as barley was needed elsewhere to support the war effort. Any hope of their revival was blighted when America, the top export market, declared Prohibition in 1920.

In addition to this, UK Excise Duty continued to rise, with the result that between 1908 and 1922 the bottle price rose from two shillings (10p) to more than 12 shillings (60p). Further misery ensued with the General Strike, the Wall Street Crash and the Great Depression – as a consequence of which the industry went into meltdown. It has been estimated that in 1890 Scotland boasted some 150 distilleries. For a few nadir months in 1933, only eight were still operating. While some reopened in the late 1930s and after the Second World War, many did not.

Ireland fared even worse. On top of the woes that afflicted Scotland, after 1922 the independent Irish Free State lost its main market, Britain. In turn, the tally of its distilleries shrank, from around 30 to

Opposite.
Devanha Distillery on the river Dee, Aberdeen, 1885.

Above.
Dundashill Distillery.

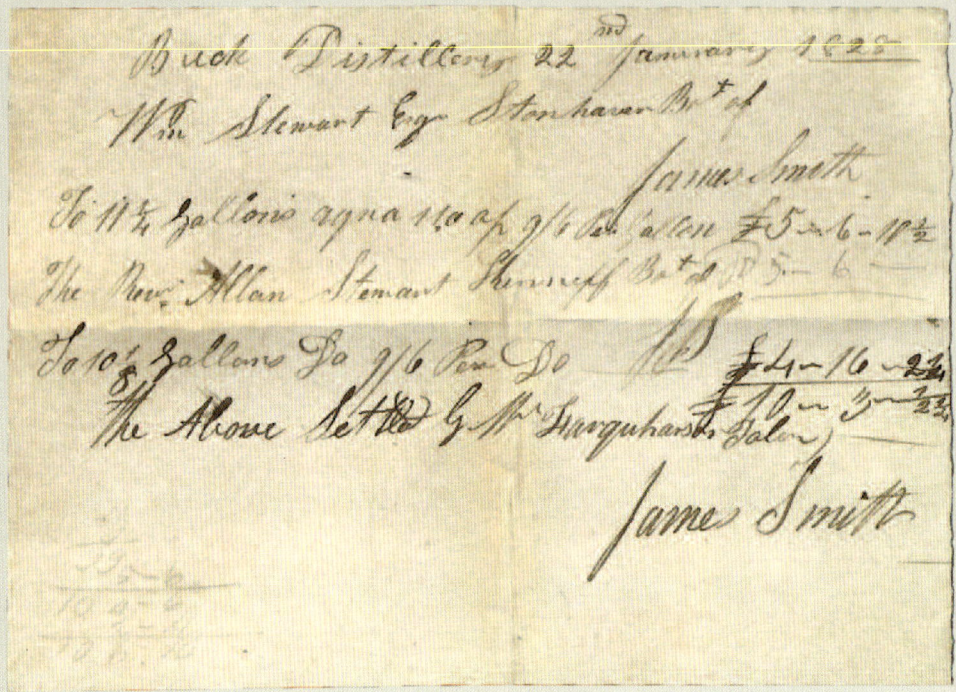

A receipt for goods from Buck Distillery in the Cabrach.

at one point just two. However, its fortunes have now revived.

With a few exceptions, the loss of Scotland's distilleries falls into four phases: the period around 1800; the decades following the 1820s and the stampede into legal distilling during which the weakest failed; the darkest period from 1900 to the early 1930s, when the effect of the temperance movement, punitive taxation, US Prohibition and the Great Depression brought the industry to its knees; and in more recent times, the 1980s, when overproduction, low demand and poor management led to the closure of some two dozen distilleries. As a result, there is no corner of Scotland that does not lament the loss of a handful (or, in the case of Campbeltown, 20) of distilleries, casualties of the shifting fortunes of the whisky industry.

The east and north-east of Scotland have suffered disproportionately, the exception being Speyside, which since 1945 has seen its distillery flock grow and prosper.

Angus (formally Kincardineshire), Banffshire and especially Aberdeenshire saw a spate of losses in all four periods, particularly between 1830 and 1850, when a swathe of distilleries folded. Most were small, undercapitalised and — until the law allowed limited liability companies — many were deeply prone to sequestration whenever a bad harvest, slow payments or distillation problems hit their cash flow.

Records show that at the end of the eighteenth century there were 14 distilleries in and around Huntly. Within a few years, virtually all had folded. Aberdeen boasted a stack of distilleries at one time or another, including Rubislaw, Don Bridge, South Bridge, Stoneytown, Broadford, Denburn, Gilcomston, Greenhaugh and Union Glen, all of which closed during the nineteenth century. Three others survived into the twentieth century — Bon Accord, Devanha and Strathdee — the former two closing before the First World War, Strathdee by the Second.

Many tiny rural distilleries in the north-east

came and went in the nineteenth century, including three in the remote and notorious illicit distilling area of the Cabrach: Tomnaven, Lesmurdie (aka Cabrach), and the curiously named Black Middens, or the Buck. Even historic Corgarff Castle on Donside briefly housed a distillery in 1826, as did at one time or another localities as varied as Aberdour, Portsoy, Monymusk, Monquhitter, New Byth, Longside, Fraserburgh, Rhynie, Peterhead, Inverurie and Muckle Wartle.

A particularly sad loss was Jericho, near Insch, which closed around 1915. Its whisky was sold as Benachie (with one 'n'), a brand successfully re-launched in the 1990s. Another brand to be resurrected is Black Bull, a blend first produced by George Willsher of Dundee, using malt from the Glen Coull distillery at Justinhaugh. Glen Coull closed around 1929, but the name Black Bull has been revived by Duncan Taylor of Huntly as a deluxe blend aged 12, 18 and 40 years.

The area's losses in the 1980s and 1990s included North Port in Brechin, Lochside and Hillside/Glenesk at Montrose, Glenury Royal at Stonehaven, Glenugie near Peterhead and lastly Banff, which survived a Luftwaffe bombing in 1941.

However, two distilleries that spent years in mothballs — Glen Garioch and Glenglassaugh — are thankfully now thriving again, along with a number of other east coast distilleries, including Glencadam at Brechin, Fettercairn, Royal Lochnagar, Glen Deveron/Macduff, An Cnoc and Glendronach, all of which are doing well.

Despite the north-east losing many of its distilleries, one can truly say the future of those that have survived looks assured.

Above.
Glenugie Distillery, Peterhead.

Left.
A nineteenth-century bottle label from Banff Distillery.

Epilogue

'Scotland has over 4,000 miles of coastline and many islands and it is vulnerable and is targeted by unscrupulous, ruthless people who peddle their trade and make vast profits. They are full of guile, subterfuge, and they are very, very difficult to catch.'

John Clifford, Assistant Chief Investigation Officer, HM Customs and Excise, 1996[1]

Smuggling in Scotland is still big business. In the spring of 2013, an operation involving more than 50 police officers and lasting two and a half years came to fruition when members of a Scottish smuggling gang were sentenced to a combined total of 51.5 years in prison. In an echo of the whisky gangs of yore, the 15-member cannabis network included experts in transport and finance, and was 'run along the lines of a conventional business'.[2] While some would see cannabis-smoking as a victimless crime, arguments to the contrary can certainly be made. Senior customs officer Alastair Soutar was crushed to death in 1996 while attempting to board the suspected cannabis boat *Ocean Jubilee* as part of Operation Balvenie: a four-cutter, 70-officer sting that netted drugs worth an estimated £8 million and resulted in 13 arrests.[3] Much of the current smuggling picture is altogether darker. In the first quarter of 2014, for instance, Scottish authorities uncovered three new cases of people-trafficking per week.[4] In fairness, the known people-smuggling cases amounted to less than 7 per cent of the UK total during the same period, but given that Scotland represents 32 per cent of the UK's landmass and has 59 per cent of her coastline,[5] this merely fuelled fears that the detected cases were the tip of an iceberg. Mostly from Eastern Europe, West Africa and East Asia, the victims were destined for sexual exploitation, slavery and/or organ harvesting.[6]

Scotland's distinct legal system and ever-changing policing framework may make it easier for drug smugglers to operate there, as compared to the rest of the UK: '[t]he time taken to provide the results of forensic analysis [of suspicious

Opposite.
The busy fishing port of Fraserburgh, historically important in offshore smuggling operations in the north-east of Scotland.

substances] in Scotland is much greater than in England and Wales'; illegal-drug possession north of the border can still be punished merely via 'fiscal fines'; and the sharing of information between Scottish police and the Home Office was patchy even before the reinstatement of the Scottish parliament in 1999.[7]

The main type of alcohol-related dodgy dealing reported in Scotland in recent years has involved counterfeiting of known brands, almost inevitably vodka, and the counterfeiting of 'duty paid' labels for bottles of genuine spirits that have been illegally diverted from export to domestic markets. The former wheeze, in particular, appears to be growing rapidly in popularity. Three out of 23 retail shops inspected by Trading Standards officers in East Ayrshire in August 2013 appeared to be engaged in one or the other of these practices; and 200 more bottles of counterfeit vodka – notable for the spelling mistakes on their labels, including 'botteled' for 'bottled' – were seized from just one shop in Moray in February 2015.[8] A single 40-foot lorry like the one seized at Cairnryan, Wigtownshire, on 26 September 2013 can hold more than 13,000 litres of fake vodka, representing a loss to the taxman of tens of thousands of pounds.[9] UK-wide, more than two million litres of such alcohol per year were seized by HMRC between 2005 and 2011. Worse, according to Drinkaware's chief medical advisor, Professor Paul Wallace, common substitutes for drinkable ethanol in such products include 'chemicals used in cleaning fluids, nail polish remover and automobile screen wash . . . antifreeze and some fuels'. These chemicals can lead to 'nausea and vomiting, abdominal pain, drowsiness and dizziness . . . kidney or liver problems . . . coma [or] permanent blindness'.[10] All of this is a stark reminder that, far from being merely a way of squeezing money out of people's 'sinful' behaviour, state oversight of the production and sale of alcohol (and a vast range of other ingestible substances) is also intended to protect public and individual health.

The romantic associations of smuggling, then, no longer apply. Modern smuggling is, perhaps, simply too ugly. The port of Fraserburgh's somewhat exaggerated reputation as a major European entrepôt for heroin is more a source of shame and fear than of local pride; and despite a strong recent resurgence of popular anti-Union sentiment – particularly in the south-west of Scotland and Dundee – such feelings seem to be expressed largely via the ballot box, and the link between them and support for smuggling that prevailed in the eighteenth century appears to be broken. Likewise, the ever-smaller world constructed by pervasive television images and the internet allows the disaffected to aim their fury directly at the House of Commons, usually in writing, rather than by cudgelling those among their neighbours who happen to work for HMRC.

Amid the resurgence of smuggling, nationalism and human slavery in the twenty-first century, the ongoing romanticisation of smugglers from the 'olden days' is a complex phenomenon. One of the very few novels written about smuggling during its heyday, Charlotte Smith's *The Old Manor House* (1793), was set during the American Revolution of two decades earlier – in part, so that its radical republican English author would not have to allude directly to her support for the French Revolution then in progress. It was read and highly praised by Sir Walter Scott, who took up the smuggling theme himself in *Guy Mannering* (1815). Ireland's answer to Scott, John Banim, wrote a novel called *The Smuggler* in 1831 and took a somewhat more sympathetic view than Scott, whose Solway free traders were kidnappers as well as murderers. Banim's book is not to be confused with G.P.R. James's *The Smuggler*, which focused on the derring-do of the gaugers, noble anti-smuggling sentiments among the 'peasantry', and the contraband traders' 'brutal crimes' and 'merited' punishments.[11] By and large, however, British fiction about smuggling was rare while the practice was still current: it came into its own only in the last decade of the nineteenth century, i.e. almost immediately after the real thing came to be considered dead and buried. Enormous success attended the publication of Kirkcudbrightshire-born Samuel Crockett's *The Raiders* in 1894 and J. Meade Falkner's *Moonfleet* in 1898. The latter was made into a feature film by the legendary Fritz Lang, and at least three television mini-series versions have followed, along with multiple radio dramatisations. Graham Greene, arguably the British author most closely attuned to the needs of the cinema, also chose a nineteenth-century smuggling plot for his first novel, *The Man Within* (1929); the inevitable film version starred Michael Redgrave and Richard Attenborough. The book ascribed a level and type of violence to its smugglers that, if not unknown in the historical record, now seems somewhat exaggerated. Greene himself later condemned the project as 'embarrassingly romantic' and 'derivative', and its commercial success as 'inexplicable'.[12] Most smuggling books of the 1890s through the interwar period featured grim litanies of murder and execution, but, in reality, deaths of smugglers caught red-handed on Scotland's shores were almost infeasibly rare – in the case of one fellow who was actually killed by the Excise near Slains, Aberdeenshire, in 1798, the officers were tried for murder.[13]

As his name suggests, Russell Thorndike's fictive Georgian smuggler-cum-supervillain Doctor Syn was a very bad man who met with a bad end, but this did nothing to blunt the commercial success of the seven lurid novels centred on his wicked exploits that were published between 1915 and 1944. The character was portrayed on film by George Arliss, Peter Cushing and Patrick McGoohan, and (parodically) by Sid James; Doctor Syn was also a character in the original comic-book version of *The League of Extraordinary Gentlemen*. Mollie Hunter's popular young adult novel *The Lothian Run* (1971), set in the 1730s, made a rare literary link between Scottish smuggling and Jacobitism, painting both in a mostly negative light – though it should be remembered that even southern

English smugglers of c.1690–1750 were frequently Jacobites or Jacobite sympathisers, as a monumental research project by Professor Paul Monod has revealed.[14] Recent British television productions including *Poldark* (2015) and *Jamaica Inn* (2014), both based on twentieth-century historical novels, have also focused on the dark, desperate and dangerous character of the enterprise in the Georgian period, but have notably failed to demonise the officers of the law in the same way as many earlier works, the Doctor Syn novels included.

One of the world's most famous and best-loved smuggling stories, however, takes place in modern times. Set in the Outer Hebrides[15] during the Second World War, Compton Mackenzie's 1947 novel *Whisky Galore* is a fictionalised, comic account of the 1941 wreck of a cargo ship full of whisky and £145,000 in cash that was pilfered by the local islanders. The story – and the immensely popular Ealing film version shot by Alexander MacKendrick on Barra in 1948 – focuses on the clever ruses used by the community to save their windfall from confiscation at the hands of a pompous English army captain. With their emphasis on wiliness, lack of violence and community *esprit de corps*, the book and film (perhaps permanently) shifted the emphasis of Scotland's whisky-smuggling heritage away from violence, intimidation and immorality. Interestingly, the film's Massachusetts-born director later mused that only the English villain seemed much like a Scotsman to him, and the rest of the characters like Irishmen.

In any case, *Whisky Galore*'s warmer, fuzzier approach was widely adopted thereafter: for instance, by popular folk-rock band The Men They Couldn't Hang, whose 1988 song 'Smugglers' was essentially the traditional Scots smuggling ballad 'The Lads of Lendalfit' translated into standard English. As Hew Ainslie's 1822 printed version had it:

'O, Mungo, ye've a cozzy bield
'Wi' a butt ay an' a ben,
'Can ye no live a lawfu' life,
'An' ligg wi' lawfu' men?'

Gae blaw your win aneth your pat,
It's blawn awa on me,
For, bag and bark, shall be my wark,
Until the day I die.

Maun I haud by our hameart goods
An' foreign gear sae fine?
Maun I drink at the water wan
An' France sae rife o' wine?

Epilogue

A Highlander attending his still.

Notably, the rock song omitted the Ainslie version's reference to violence against a gauger and added an invented *Whisky Galore*-ish final stanza in which the parson and church congregation are shown as complicit in the transport and concealment of the goods. It would be hard to find a clearer-cut example of how the figure of the Scottish smuggler in fiction has been subtly 'whitewashed' over the past 200 years.

In the post-Second World War period, as excise taxes made up an ever-dwindling proportion of the state's revenue base, and Church-led campaigns against the 'demon drink' came to seem almost as much a thing of the past as pony-trains, straightforward condemnations of historical smuggling on legal or moral grounds became extremely rare. But this may now change. Not long after the release of Danny Boyle's hit Edinburgh drug-world tragicomedy *Trainspotting* (1996), BBC Two's *The Fast Show* aired a brilliant and disturbing parody of *Whisky Galore!*, called *Heroin Galore!* More recently, Steve Hudson's feature film *True North* (2006) presented a grim, blood-soaked tale of people-trafficking of Mainland Chinese into Britain from Belgium via a Peterhead-registered fishing trawler. These current shifts in the wind make it a very different atmosphere into which Gillies MacKinnon's remake of *Whisky Galore!*, starring Eddie Izzard as the army officer, and which was filmed at the early smuggling port of Portsoy on the Moray Firth, premiered. But it is at least possible that the fundamental legality and social acceptance of whisky-drinking, in contrast to both drug-taking and slave-trading, will allow us as a culture to permanently compartmentalise the smuggling of it in its own mist-shrouded Brigadoon.

Endnotes

The Illicit Distilling and Smuggling of Whisky

I A Nation of Smugglers

1. Until the late eighteenth century, official and unofficial documents referred to distilled spirits as *aqua vitae* or *aquavite*, Latin for 'water of life'. The word 'whisky' comes from the Gaelic for 'water of life', *uisge beatha* (pronounced 'ooshky-bayaha'). Progressively it was anglicised from 'uiskie' (1618) to 'whiskie' (1715), then 'usky' (1736). By 1746, we have 'whisky'.
2. Thomas Tucker, *Report Upon the Settlement of the Revenues of Excise and Customs in Scotland* (1656; first printed in Edinburgh, 1825), pp. 16–17.
3. Duncan Fraser, *The Smugglers* (Montrose, 1971) pp. 89–90.

II Union and Disorder

4. Some of the causes of famines are quite fascinating. The 1816 famine – 'the year without summer' – resulting in British crop failures for another three years, was due to the northern atmospheric diffusion of ash from the Tambora volcano in Indonesia. It started its eruptions in April 1815.

III Ancient Liberties

5. This is the first record we have of the 'progress of the [licensed] trade'.
6. The measure of liquid in a hogshead varied according to the liquid, from 46 imperial gallons for claret and Madeira to 57 gallons for port and brandy. Ultimately the measure stabilised at 52.5 gallons (238.5 litres) for wine and 54 gallons (250 litres) for beer and whisky.
7. Account Books of Broomhall Estate. I am grateful to Lord Elgin for this information.
8. Gavin D. Smith, *The Scottish Smuggler* (Edinburgh, 2003), p. 8.
9. Fraser, *The Smugglers*, p. 97, quoting the Customs House Records of Montrose.

10. Quoted by Charles H. Craig, *The Scotch Whisky Industry Record* (Dumbarton, 1995), p. 36.
11. Edward Burt, *Letters from a Gentleman in the North of Scotland to his Friend in London,* 5th edition (London, 1754; 1822) vol. I, p. 134.
12. Edward Burt, *Letters from a Gentleman in the North of Scotland*, vol. II, p 161 and p. 163.

IV Open Transgression

13. John Scott, *A Paper on the Means of Suppressing Smuggling in the Distillery of Scotland* (Edinburgh, 1784), quoted by Michael S. Moss and John R. Hume, *The Making of Scotch Whisky* (Edinburgh, 1981), p. 36.
14. Michael S. Moss and John R. Hume, *The Making of Scotch Whisky*, p. 36.
15. Duncan Forbes of Culloden, quoted by Smith, *The Scottish Smuggler*, pp. 15–16.
16. Moss and Hume, *The Making of Scotch Whisky,* p. 45.
17. David Bremner, *The Industries of Scotland* (Edinburgh, 1869) pp. 444–54, reprinted in *Whisky Words*, Aaron Barker (ed.) (Carmel, Indiana, 2015), pp. 24–34.
18. George Bishop, *Observations, Remarks and Means to Prevent Smuggling* (Maidstone, 1783), quoted in Smith, *The Scottish Smuggler*, p. 19.
19. H. Grey Graham, *The Social Life of Scotland in the Eighteenth Century* (Edinburgh, 1899), quoted in Smith, *The Scottish Smuggler*, p. 20.
20. Ian Macdonald, *Smuggling in the Highlands* (Stirling, 1914), p. 99.
21. ibid., p. 100.
22. Vivien E. Dietz, 'The Politics of Whisky: Scottish Distillers, the Excise, and the Pittite State', *Journal of British Studies*, 36(1) (1997), p. 50.

V Distilling in a Thousand Hands

23. Quoted by Moss and Hume, *The Making of Scotch Whisky*, p. 51. It was claimed that in some places stills of 80 gallons' capacity could be 'worked off, emptied and ready for another operation in three and a half minutes, sometimes in three minutes', but this seems scarcely credible (see Macdonald, *Smuggling in the Highlands*, p. 54).
24. Charles H. Craig, *The Scotch Whisky Industry Record* (Dumbarton, 1994), p. 58.
25. *Report of a Select Committee of the House of Commons 1798*, quoted in David Daiches, *Scotch Whisky* (London, 1969), p. 34.
26. Rev. David Dunoon's entry in the *Statistical Account of Scotland* (1791–99).
27. John Leydon, *A Tour in the Highlands and Western Islands* (London, 1800)
28. Rev. David Dunoon's entry in the *Statistical Account of Scotland* (1791–99).
29. Lord Justice Clerk Granton, quoted by Malcolm Archibald, *Whisky Wars, Riots and Murder* (Edinburgh 2013), p. 16.
30. Stephen W. Sillett, *Illicit Scotch* (Aberdeen, 1965), p. 29.
31. Quoted by Gavin Smith, *The Secret Still* (Edinburgh, 2002), p.73.
32. Quoted by Derek Cooper and Fay Godwin, *The Whisky Roads of Scotland* (London, 1982) p. 30.

Endnotes

33. Moss and Hume, *The Making of Scotch Whisky.*
34. Thomas Guthrie D.D., *Autobiography* (Edinburgh, 1874), quoted in Craig, *The Scotch Whisky Industry Record*, p. 67–8.
35. Alfred Barnard, *The Whisky Distilleries of the United Kingdom* (London, 1887), p. 149.
36. Bremner, *The Industries of Scotland.*
37. Cooper and Godwin, *The Whisky Roads of Scotland*, p. 39.
38. James Mackay, *A Biography of Robert Burns* (Edinburgh, 1992) p. 449 and p. 450.
39. Osgood Hanbury Mackenzie, *A Hundred Years in the Highlands* (London, 1921), p.218, quoting Dr John Mackenzie.
40. William Alexander, *Notes and Sketches Illustrative of Northern Rural Life* (Aberdeen, 1877), quoted by Sillett, *Illicit Scotch*, p. 41.
41. Sillett, *Illicit Scotch*, p. 42.
41. Bremner, *The Industries of Scotland.*
43. Samuel Morewood, *The Manufacture and Use of Inebriating Liquors* (Dublin, 1824), p. 474.

VI Carrot and Stick

44. Barnard, *The Whisky Distilleries of the United Kingdom*, p. 57.
45. William P. Coyne (ed.), *Ireland; Industrial and Agricultural* (Dublin, 1902) p. 502, quoted by Aaron Barker in *Whisky Words* (Carmel, Indiana, 2015), p. 58.
46. Ross Wilson, *Scotch: Its History and Romance* (Newton Abbot, 1973), p. 58, quoting an unnamed newspaper.
47. Moss and Hume, *The Making of Scotch Whisky*, p. 83, quoting the *Ardchattan MS.*
48. T.C. Smout, *A Century of the Scottish People 1830–1950* (London, 1986), p. 134, quoting John Dunlop, *The Philosophy of Artificial and Compulsory Drinking Usage* (London, 1839).
49. *Harper's Manual 1915*, quoted by Craig, *The Scotch Whisky Industry Record*, p. 107.
50. Sillet, *Illicit Scotch*, pp. 69–70.
51. Income tax had first been levied by William Pitt in 1797 to pay for the war with France, and abandoned in 1816.
52. Quoted by Gavin Smith, p.25
53. *Harper's Manual* 1915, p.107.
54. Scottish duties were gradually increased between 1853 and 1855 to match those in England.
55. Charles Tovey, *British and Foreign Spirits* (London, 1864), p. 150.

VII The Last Gasps

56. Macdonald, *Smuggling in the Highlands*, p. 7.
57. Archibald, *Whisky Wars*, pp. 29–30.
58. Sillet, *Illicit Scotch*, p. 106.
59. During the 1920s the Land League fully merged with the Labour Party, with the promise of Scotland being granted autonomy in the event of a Labour victory.

Smuggling's Heartland: The Cabrach

I A Raiding Base on the Highland Line

1. It is anticipated that similar long-term case studies of other areas of the country, such as the Isle of Islay, would yield equally interesting results.
2. Including Terpersie, Knockespock, Cocklarachie, Prony, and Newtoun, along with at least one son of Gordon of Lesmoir, one of the richest men in the country, whose daughter Katherine married the laird of Leys c.1594, thereby becoming the first mistress of the magnificent Crathes Castle on Deeside.
3. Barry Robertson, *Lordship and Power in the North of Scotland: The Noble House of Huntly, 1603–1690* (Edinburgh, 2011), p. 31.
4. Greatly extended and 'facelifted' almost beyond recognition, this house is now known as Reekimlane. For the date of the battle, we have accepted C.O. Skelton and J.M. Bulloch, *Gordons Under Arms* (Aberdeen, 1912), p. 105, though other authors have assigned it to 1592. The ballad quotation is as reported in Douglas Wimberley, 'Some Notes on the Cabrach', Aberdeen University MS LA F 4 Wim, fo.[16].
5. He was a collateral ancestor of the Gordons of Pitlurg, who included the famous cartographers Gordon of Straloch (1580–1661) and Gordon of Rothiemay (1617–86), as well as Gordon of Auchleuchries, one of Imperial Russia's most famous generals (d. 1699).
6. *Sheriff Court Records – Aberdeen*, ed. David Littlejohn (Aberdeen, 1906), Vol. 1, pp. 202 and 257–9. The Gordon families of Lesmoir and Beldornie had both taken part in Huntly's unsuccessful, ultra-Catholic rebellion against the more moderate Mary, Queen of Scots in 1562.
7. Of the remainder, in 1610, seven were occupied exclusively by commoners and four were unoccupied.
8. Arthur Johnston (c.1579–1641), quoted in the editor's notes to James Gordon of Rothiemay, *History of Scots Affairs, From 1637 to 1641* (Aberdeen, 1841), appendix to editor's preface, p. ii.
9. Commission to the Marquis of Huntly, Edinburgh, 19 March 1635, quoted in full in John Spalding's *Memorialls* (1850 edition), Vol. 1, pp. 425–7, quotation at p. 426. All spellings have been modernised.

II Nursery of the Royalist Cavalry

10. Records of the Parliaments of Scotland (hereafter 'RPS'), 1649/1/381 (16 March 1649).

III The Campbells Triumphant and the Coming of Smuggling

11. Scottish legislators cited 'the present marching of the army': RPS 1644/1/48. RPS 1644/1/65 (31 January 1644) was initially an emergency measure designed by the revolutionary covenanting state to expire by February 1645, but the excise system

it had created was extended first until 1 August 1645, and second until 1 January 1648 by RPS 1644/6/283 (29 July 1644) and RPS 1646/11/329 (10 March 1647). The last-named act mentioned that imported spirits, 'in respect the same is prohibited and ought to be confiscated', were taxed at the higher rate of 6s 8d per pint. A Scots pint equalled a little over 2.8 English pints.

12. Although this is often hailed as a first by whisky authors, it should perhaps be acknowledged that Edinburgh and Leith were allowed to collect *local* excise taxes, on wine, at the rate of £4 Scots per tun, beginning in 1609 and 1612, respectively: RPS 1621/6/3.
13. See Patrick Gordon, *Britane's Distemper*; Sir William Fraser, *The Melvilles, Earls of Melville, and the Leslies, Earls of Leven*, vol. 2, p. 96; *Act. Parl. Scot.*, vol. 6 pt. 1, p. 723; *Act. Parl. Scot.*, vol. 6 pt. 2, p. 738; W. Gordon, *History of the Family of Gordon* (1727).
14. *Extracts from the Presbytery Book of Strathbogie 1631–1654* (Aberdeen, 1843), pp. 39, 75.
15. David Calderwood, *The History of the Kirk of Scotland*, ed. Thomas Thomson (Edinburgh, 1843), Vol. 4, pp. 658–9.
16. National Records of Scotland (hereafter 'NAS') GD44/51/739/63-70; NAS GD44/51/75/2.
17. Robertson, *Lordship and Power*, p. 167.
18. RPS C1681/7/23.

IV Resistance Continues: The Ferintosh Years

19. A further indication of the strength of the Campbell–Forbes–Clan Chattan alliance that was ranged against the House of Gordon for generation after generation.
20. Even aside from the aforementioned roasting of Margaret Campbell, the sixteenth-century Gordon vs Forbes feud is the stuff of extremely gory legend; and it was no coincidence that John, 8th Lord Forbes, was second-in-command of Argyll's Protestant forces at the above mentioned Battle of Glenlivet.
21. Gaelic was 'commonly spoken, and universally understood' in Ferintosh and environs as late as the 1790s.
22. Alexander Murdoch, 'Argathelians (*act.* 1705–*c.*1765)', *Oxford Dictionary of National Biography* online edition (hereafter '*ODNB*'), accessed 8 January 2015.
23. Duncan Fraser, *The Smugglers* (Montrose, 1978), p. 9.
24. Paul Monod, 'Dangerous Merchandise: Smuggling, Jacobitism, and Commercial Culture in Southeast England, 1690–1760', *Journal of British Studies* 30(2) (April 1991), pp. 150–82, p. 171.
25. Guy Chaussinand-Nogaret, 'Une elite insulaire au service de l'Europe: Les Jacobites au XVIIIe siecle', *Annales* 20 (1973), pp. 1,098–9; Jan Parmentier, 'The Sweets of Commerce: the Hennessys of Ostend and their Network in the Eighteenth Century', in David Dickson *et al.*, eds, *Irish and Scottish Mercantile Networks in Europe and Overseas in the Seventeenth and Eighteenth Centuries* (Ghent, 2006), pp. 67–92; W.A. Cole, 'Trends in Eighteenth-Century Smuggling', *Economic History Review*, New Series 10(3) (1958), pp. 395–410, p. 407; Monod,

'Dangerous Merchandise', p. 164 (from which the quotation).
26. NAS CE87/1/1, 23 June 1729.
27. *Some Considerations on the Present State of Scotland* (Edinburgh: W. Sands, 28 March 1744), pp. 5–6.
28. Monod, 'Dangerous Merchandise', p. 159.
29. *The Spirit of Loyalty, and of Rebellion, During some late Troubles, Detected, In the Conduct of the Commissioners of Excise in Scotland* (Westminster: H. Griffiths, 1755), pp. 15–17.
30. A key example is Capt. John Gordon of the 92nd Foot, later laird of Coynachie, who worked extensively as a recruiting officer after 1778, mostly in the Cabrach and Strathbogie; he was the son of John Gordon from Auchmair, Cabrach (1701–52), a Jacobite soldier in the '45 who was 'treated with great rigour' by the authorities. See J.M. Bulloch, *Territorial Soldiering in the North-East of Scotland during 1759–1814* (Aberdeen, 1914), pp. 45 ff., and Wimberley, 'Some Notes', fos. [14], [19].
31. Or at any rate, the contraband item most frequently intercepted by the authorities.
32. T.M. Devine, *Clanship to Crofters' War: The social transformation of the Scottish Highlands* (Manchester, 1994), p. 126.

V A Logic of Its Own: From Smuggling to Distilling, 1760 to 1790

33. The Beldornie Gordons descended from one of several illegitimate sons of Adam Gordon, dean of Caithness and third son of the 1st Earl of Huntly (d. 1470). The Alexander Gordon who moved into Beldornie Castle in 1700 brought with him his wife Sìleas nighean Mhic Raghnaill (*c.*1660–*c.*1729), well-known Gaelic poet of the Jacobite rising of 1715. James Gordon, 6th laird of Letterfourie in Rathven, and his brother Alexander were Jacobites who set up a wine business on Madeira – a globally important centre of smuggling – in 1742. The height of their success there, 1742–60, coincides almost exactly with the introduction of brandy as a madeira wine ingredient, which was first suggested in print in 1743, and general practice by 1760.
34. Rev. James Gordon, *OSA* for Cabrach.
35. In the summer of 1775: see NAS CE4/1, Scottish Excise, Board to Collectors, 1775–1791, pp. 1–7.
36. General Letter to Collectors, 31 July 1797, NAS CE4/2, p. 84.
37. Aberdeen City Archives (hereafter 'ACA'), Minute Book Commissioners of Supply, Banffshire, 1773–1789, p. 191; NAS CE4/2, Scottish Excise, Board to Collectors, 1791–1804, 'Instructions to Mr. Alexr. Malcolm[,] Riding Supervisor on the Distillery & Spirit Smuggling': p. 242 [26 January 1802].
38. Vivien E. Dietz, 'The Politics of Whisky: Scottish Distillers, the Excise, and the Pittite State', *Journal of British Studies* 36(1) (1997), pp. 35–69, p. 50; Gordon, *OSA* for Cabrach.

Endnotes

VI After the Ferintosh: Cabrach Smuggling's Golden Age

39. Series of newspaper articles written by William Thomson in 1909 and 1910, published in the *Weekly Scotsman*, the *Kilmarnock Standard*, and the *Inverness Courier* newspapers, and preserved in the British Library as BL 08227 b22, fos. [10–10v], [24], [26] and [28v]; Jean Pike, *Scottish Smugglers* (St Ives, 1975), pp. 3–5.
40. On 6 February 1827. *Proceedings*, pp. 245–6.
41. *Aberdeen Journal*, issue 3,780, 21 June 1820. Not this, but a similar incident probably led to a 'Large Quantity' of Highland whisky being offered for sale by auction at the Permit Office in Netherkirkgate: *Aberdeen Journal*, issue 3,762, 16 February 1820.
42. Joseph Mitchell, *Reminiscences of My Life in the Highlands* (Newton Abbot, 1971), Vol. 2, p. 35. Mitchell once came upon a pony-train of 25 ponies with a dozen guards armed with bludgeons: *ibid*., p. 61.
43. Letter from George Gordon, solicitor, to an unknown clergyman, 1 June 1825, NAS GD44/51/433/90.
44. Pike, *Scottish Smugglers*, p. 30
45. See, for example, *Aberdeen Journal* issue 4,110 (18 October 1826); issue 4,269 (4 November 1829); and issue 4,581 (28 October 1835). Clark eventually added merely 'Good' whisky to his repertoire, at 6s 6d to 7s 6d a gallon, while the prices for 'Fine' and Cabrach remained unchanged: *Aberdeen Journal*, issue 4,274 (9 December 1829).
46. Issue 15,871, 24 May 1823.
47. Parliamentary Papers VII, 1823, *Fifth Report . . . Public Revenue*, p. 427, quoted in Devine, *Clanship*, p. 127.
48. *Trial of Malcolm Gillespie*, p. 38.
49. We have found no interruption in Gordon occupation of Largue from 1610 onward into the nineteenth century; and a leading Gordon historian has remarked that '[t]here can be few places in Great Britain where farms have been held so generally by members of the same family, from father to son' than Cabrach: Wimberley, 'Some Notes', fo. [14]. On Cocklarachie's wealth in 1643, see http://bellcomm01.uuhost. uk.uu.net/history/landownership.htm (accessed 27 January 2015).
50. NAS, *Crim'l Letters . . . Ag't Alexander Gordon 1823*, pp. 2–3.
51. Ibid., pp. 4–5.
52. Ibid., p. 6.
53. Ibid., p. 7, 9
54. NAS, Alexander Gordon's statement to William Kennedy, 1822, pp. 1–2.
55. *Edinburgh Advertiser* (1823), p. 264.
56. NAS JC11/70/84r (on 21 April 1826); NAS JC11/74/102r (on 8 September 1828); NAS JC11/82/42v (on 29 April 1834). An Alexander Gordon was also prosecuted on 23 September 1819 because 'Malt was found privately making in one of defendant's barns', but was discharged without trial on payment of £20 – despite the prosecution having cost more than £40 up to that point.

VII Passing into History?

57. *Aberdeen Journal* no. 4,868, 28 April 1841.
58. Douglas Wimberley, *A Short Family History of the Later Gordons of Beldorney* (Banff, 1904), p. 24.
59. Rosa Elena's maternal grandfather was James Arthur Gordon of Jerez: ibid., p. 24, 27
60. Sillett, *Illicit Scotch*, p. 72, 74, 75, 98, quotations all at p. 75.
61. Ian MacDonald, *Smuggling in the Highlands: An Account of Highland Whisky with Smuggling Stories and Detections* (Stirling, 1914), p. 121.
62. 'A Huntly Appeal Case', *Aberdeen Journal*, 29 October 1890, p. 7.
63. Gavin Smith, *The Secret Still* (Edinburgh, 2002), p. 87.
64. Illicit Distilling', *Aberdeen Journal*, 14 May 1906, p. 5
65. 'Illicit Still Fines: Secret of An Underground Cellar', *Gloucestershire Echo*, 8 January 1934, p. 1.
66. 'Dinnet Audience Enjoys Comedy', *Aberdeen Journal*, 19 March 1934, p. 9.
67. 'Caithness Trafficking Fine of £75', *Aberdeen Journal*, 6 April 1928, p. 10.
68. 'Illicit Distilling in North', *Aberdeen Journal*, 17 August 1922, p. 6; 'Fined £100 for Illicit Distilling', *Aberdeen Journal*, 14 November 1928, p. 7; 'Illicit Distiller Fined', *Aberdeen Journal*, 3 August 1927, p. 7.
69. 'Another Whisky Cut Feared', *Aberdeen Journal*, 29 January 1947, p. 3.
70. 'William Russell's Passing Glances', *Aberdeen Journal*, 29 October 1947, p. 2.
71. Sillett, *Illicit Scotch*, pp. 109–17.
72. For one of the numerous examples of this stereotyped view, see Dietz, 'Politics of Whisky', pp. 46–7.
73. Devine, *Clanship to Crofters' War*, p. 129. Unlike Professor Devine, the excise service itself seemed quite aware that persons who distilled whisky illicitly in the Highland Zone could also be 'themselves Dealers in the Lowlands': Board to all Collectors, 16 June 1815, at p. 293 in NAS CE4/3, Scottish Excise, Board to Collectors, 1804–18.
74. L.M. Cullen, 'The Smuggling Trade in Ireland in the Eighteenth Century', *Proceedings of the Royal Irish Academy*, Vol. 67 (1969), pp. 149–75.

Epilogue

1. 'Operation that Cost Customs Officer His Life Had Been Going on at International Level For Months; Nine Charged after Sea Drama', *The Herald* online, 31 July 1996, accessed 20 December 2015.
2. Gareth Rose, '50 Years in Jail for "Biggest" Scots Drug Gang', *The Scotsman* online, 28 April 2013, accessed 17 December 2015.
3. 'Operation that Cost Customs Officer His Life'.
4. Keith McLeod, 'Three Cases of Human Trafficking Discovered in Scotland Every Week amid Concerns Many More Are Going Undetected', *Daily Record* online, 20/31 August 2014, accessed 17 December 2015.

Endnotes

5. If the major outlying islands of all four nations are included. If dealing with the British mainland only, Scotland's percentage is around 38 per cent: www.cartography.org.uk/default.asp?content ID=749.
6. McLeod, 'Cases of Human Trafficking'.
7. Home Office/Office of National Statistics, *National Statistics Quality Review Report No. 29: Review of Drug Seizure and Offender Statistics* (London and Cardiff, 2004), pp. 26 and 28.
8. 'Fake Vodka Seized in Swoops on East Ayrshire Shops', *Daily Record* online, 30 August 2013; John Robertson, '200 Bottles of Fake Vodka Seized from Moray Shop', *Press and Journal* online, 19 February 2015; and www.foodmanufacture.co.uk/Manufacturing/Fake-vodka-on-sale-in-UK, all accessed 21 December 2015.
9. 'Counterfeit Alcohol Seized at Cairnryan', 1 October 2013, www.bbc.co.uk/news/uk-scotland-south-scotland-24357069, accessed 21 December 2015.
10. 'The Dangers of Fake Alcohol', www.drinkaware.co.uk, accessed 21 December 2015.
11. G.P.R. James, *The Smuggler: A Tale* (London, 1845), Vol. 1, p. vii.
12. http://badcatholic-eclecticreader.blogspot.nl/2010/11/graham-greenes-man-within.html, accessed 30 December 2015.
13. Daniel MacCannell, *Lost Banff and Buchan* (Edinburgh, 2012), p. 183.
14. Paul Monod, 'Dangerous Merchandise: Smuggling, Jacobitism, and Commercial Culture in Southeast England, 1690–1760', *Journal of British Studies* 30(2) (April 1991), pp. 150–82. See also W.A. Cole, 'Trends in Eighteenth-Century Smuggling', *Economic History Review*, New Series 10(3) (1958), pp. 395–410, esp. pp. 408–9. However, others argue (directly against Cole) that 'the quantitative importance of smuggling during the eighteenth century is irretrievably lost': Hoh-Cheung and Lorna H. Mui, '"Trends in Eighteenth-Century Smuggling" Reconsidered', *Economic History Review*, New Series 28(1) (1975), pp. 28–43, p. 43. Others still, beginning with Cdr Lord Teignmouth in the Victorian era, have suggested only that 'the installing of the Dutchmen and Hanoverians involved the country in vast enterprises of a warlike sort, and in a National Debt; and it, by the appalling exaction of the Customs, elevated import smuggling from a more or less casual occupation into a profession and a fine art': *The Smugglers*, Vol. 1 (London, 1973 (1892)), p. 7.
15. The geography of its fictitious islands, Great Todday and Little Todday, was based on that of Barra and Eriskay, though Mackenzie took the liberty of making Great Todday a majority-Protestant island: both the real islands are Catholic.

Acknowledgements

Many thanks to William Grant and Sons, who sponsored, supported and provided illustrative material for this project. Thanks also to the staff at Birlinn Ltd, in particular Hugh Andrew, Andrew Simmons and Deborah Warner, for their help with this publication, to Gemma Cook/Cruickshank, who assisted in developing and editing this book, and to Peter and Grant Gordon for their continuing support and assistance.

The individuals and organisations that have provided and assisted in securing illustrative material include: the personnel of the Aberdeen City Archives; Aberdeen City Library; Aboyne Library; the Banff Preservation and History Society; Jim and Linda Brown of the Scotch Whisky Archive; the British Museum; the Burns Museum; Chivas Brothers; Peter Donaldson, Steve Dornan; Karen Ellington; Andrew Fairgreave; Kieran German; Phyllis Goodall; David Hayes; Veronika Krausas; Eleanor MacCannell; Alistair Mason; the National Archives of the United Kingdom; the National Galleries of Scotland; the National Library of Scotland; Stuart Petrie; Barry Robertson; SCRAN; Paul Shanks; Neil Sheed; Steve Sillett; the University of Aberdeen's Archive Collections; David Walker; and Julian Watson.

Thanks to photographers Peter Harvey of Speyside Images, David Langan, Michael Cox, Steven Tuckwell and Chris Callaway.

Permissions

Frontispiece: Chivas Brothers; vi: Aberdeen Art Gallery & Museums Collections; xii–1: James Drummond, *The Porteous Mob*, the National Galleries of Scotland; 2: Oliver Cromwell © the National Galleries of Scotland; 3: © Dumfries & Galloway Council, Nithsdale Museums; 4: HM Customs & Excise, Greenock; 5: Domenico Beccafumi, *Distillation. One of Ten Prints on the various operations of alchemy*, the National Galleries of Scotland; 6: © National Portrait Gallery, London; 7: Andrew Fairgrieve; 8: (left) Martin M303 (right) Andrew Fairgrieve; 10–11: The Art Archive/Alamy Stock Photo; 12: douglasmack; 13: Sir David Wilkie *Three Figures Sitting Round a Table, a Fourth Entering the Door*. Study for the Painting 'Smugglers Offering Run Goods for Sale or Concealment', the National Galleries of Scotland; 15: detail of James Drummond, *The Porteous Mob*, the National Galleries of Scotland; 16: Marc Ellington private collection; 17: Marc Ellington private collection; 19: Lebrecht Music and Arts Photo Library/Alamy Stock Photo; 21: Diane Sutherland; 22–3: William Grant & Sons; 26: Library of Congress, Geography and Map Division; 27: Charles Napier Hemy (England, b.1841, d.1917), *Smugglers: 'To save their necks'* 1889–1903, oil on paper on canvas, 107.9 x 213 cm, Art Gallery of New South Wales, Purchased 1906, Photo: AGNSW 4531; 28: Nicolaes Visscher, *Exactissima Regni Scotiae tabula tam in sepentrionalem et meriodionalem . . .* (1689). Reproduced by permission of the Trustees of the National Library of Scotland; 30: © Historic Environment Scotland; 33: © CSG CIC Glasgow Museums and Libraries Collections; 35: Peter Harvey, Speyside Images www.speysideimages.co.uk; 36: Peter Harvey, Speyside Images www.speysideimages.co.uk; 38–9: © CSG CIC Glasgow Museums and Libraries Collections; 41: Courtesy of Border Force National Museum; 42: © Courtesy of the Trustees of Burns Monument and Burns Cottage; 47: Alexander Nasmyth, *Robert Burns, 1759–1796. Poet*, the National Galleries of Scotland; 48–9: William Stewart Watson, *The Inauguration of Robert Burns as Poet Laureate of the Lodge*, the National Galleries of Scotland; 52: Pictorial Press Ltd/Alamy Stock Photo; 56: (bottom) Jaroslav Sekeres; 59: HM Customs and Excise, Greenock; 60–1: William Grant & Sons; 65: School of Scottish Studies, Edinburgh University; 66: Am Baile; 67: Marc Ellington private collection; 68: © St Andrews University Library; 71: © North Ayrshire Council Museums Service; 72–3: Jim Laws/Alamy Stock Photo; 74: Peter Harvey, Speyside Images www.speysideimages.co.uk; 76: National Library of Scotland; 78: Peter Harvey, Speyside Images www.speysideimages.co.uk; 81: Marc Ellington private collection; 84: © Edinburgh City Libraries; 88–9 Iain Bain Photography; 91: Photo © Julian

Paren (cc-by-sa/2.0); 93: Peter Harvey, Speyside Images www.speysideimages.co.uk; 94–5: Royal Collection Trust © Her Majesty Queen Elizabeth II, 2014/Bridgeman Images; 96: Marc Ellington private collection; 98–9: © National Maritime Museum, Greenwich, London; 101: Andrew Wright; 105: Image courtesy of Aberdeenshire Councils Museums Service; 111: Image courtesy of Aberdeenshire Councils Museums Service; 113: Image courtesy of Aberdeenshire Councils Museums; 119: Marc Ellington private collection; 122: courtesy of Jim and Linda Brown; 123: (right) courtesy of Jim and Linda Brown; 128: Georgethefourth

Index

Aberdeen Journal 106, 116, 118
agriculture
Agricultural Revolution 20, 24
    communal nature of 9
    harvest failures, famine and 29
Ainslie, Hew 128–9
Alford, Battle of 83, 86
Allardyce, Aberdeen Collector of Customs 97
American War of Independence 102
    Queen Anne 10, 91
Aqua-Vitae 3
Archibald, Malcolm 65–6
Argyll, Archibald, 3rd Duke of 11, 16
Argyll, Campbells of 75, 77–8, 79, 80, 83, 85–7, 90, 91, 100
Arliss, George 127
Armour, Jean 50
Armstrong, Robert, Peterhead coastguard 108
Arnot, Hugo 24
Attenborough, Richard 127
Atterbury Plot (1722-23) 16
Auchindoun 57, 77, 83, 93
Auldearn, Battle of 83

Baez, Joan 70
Baird William 113
Banff, smuggler's royal burgh 109–13
Banim, John 127
Banks O'Dee Distillery, Aberdeen 57
Barnard, Alfred 37–40, 51–2
Battle of the Braes 63–4
Beddoe, Alfred 70
Bedlord, Earl of 2

Beigbeider, Maria del Carmen 115
Birnie, A.R. 118
Bishop, George 25, 34
Boswell, James 19
Boyle, Danny 129
Bremner, David 24, 40–41
Broomhall Estate account books 13–14
Burns, Robert 42, 43, 69, 71
    bard and bottle 47–50
Burt, Captain Edward 15

Cabrach, barony and lands of the 8, 35, 116, 118, 122–3
census returns (1841 and 1851) 114
    dangerous frontier country 77
    European drinks trade and, kinks between 115
    golden age of smuggling in 103–8
    Gordon-Campbell rivalry in 75, 85–7
    Highland-isation of society in 85
    illicit distilling in, emergence of 100–102
    illicit distilling in, industrial scale of 93
    lawmen-cum-thieves in 80–82
    military support for excise service in 57–8, 80
    'no man's land' 78
    population of, social standing of 82
    raiding base 75–82
    Roman Catholicism of people of 83
    Royalist cavalry, nursery of 83–4
    smuggling district 52–3, 55, 75, 93, 97, 100–102
    strategic importance to Gordons of Huntly 79
    subdivision of 78–9
Caledonian Mercury 103, 106
Campbell, Archibald, 8th Earl of Argyll 83

Campbell, Colonel Alexander 58
Campbell of Lorne, Archibald 86
Campbell of Shawfield, Daniel, MP 12, 92
Carpenter, James Madison 69
Carter, James 118
Cato Street Conspiracy (1820) 51
Caulfield, William 12
Cawdor Estate, distillery at 54
Charles Fyfe & Co. of Aberdeen 106
Charles I 2, 83, 84, 86
Charles II 3, 86–7
Christie & Mitchell of Aberdeen 105–6
Churchill, Sir Winston 62
Civil War 84, 90
Clan Chattan 77–8
Clark, William, grocer in Aberdeen 106
Clifford, John, HM Customs and Excise 125
Cooper, David 110–11
Cooper, Derek 41
Cope, Sir John 14
Corgarff and Corgarff Castle 37, 56, 57, 77, 114, 123
Corn Laws, repeal of (1846) 121
Coupar, Lord James 83
Covenant and Covenanters 2, 83–4, 86
Coyne, William P. 53
Cramond, William 109, 110–11, 113
Crockett, Samuel 127
Crofters' Holdings (Scotland) Act (1886) 63, 65
Cromwell, Oliver 2–3
Culloden, Battle of 92–3, 94–5
Cumming, Ellen and John of Cardow farm, Knockando 35
Cushing, Peter 127

Darien, disaster of 9, 96
distillation process 7–8
distilleries, losses of (and resurrections) 122–3
    see also illicit distilleries
droving 9–10
Duff, James, Banff merchant 113
Duff, Margaret 113
Dunlop, John 58
Dunlop, Mrs Francis Anna Wallace (correspondent with Burns) 42
Dylan, Bob 70

Elgin, Thomas Bruce, 7th Earl of 13–14

Eunson, Magnus ('Mansie') 37–40
excise 2
    'gaugers' (measurers, evaluators of duties due) 3–4, 27, 35–6, 40–41, 43, 54, 97, 120m 127, 129
    officers of 3–4
    reality of life for excisemen 42–3
    revenues anticipated from (1655) 3
    riding officers 42–3, 57
Excise Act (1660) 3–4
    smuggling operations resulting from 4–6
Excise Act (1814) 46
Excise Act (1823) 54, 120–21
Excyse Act (1644) 2

Falkner, J. Meade 127
Ferintosh, distillery at 4, 21–2, 30, 75, 90–91, 102
Fife, Lord or first Earl (1765) 112, 113
Findlay, James 110
Forbes, Duncan, MP 90
Forbes, John, Aberdeen Collector of Taxes 110
Forbes, John, Provost of Inverness 90
Forbes of Culloden, Duncan 4, 13, 20–21, 91, 92, 93
Forbes of Culloden, John 'Bumper' 13, 20
Forbes of Towie, Margaret 77
Fraser, Duncan 2, 6
Fraser of Brackla, Captain William 54

George I 10, 14
George II 14
George III 100
George IV 106
Gillespie, Malcolm 43–4
Gladstone, William Ewart 62
Glen Coull distillery, Justinhaugh 123
Glenfiddich 57, 83
Glenlivet smuggling district 36–7, 41, 52–3, 55, 106
Glenrinnes smuggling district 55
Glorious Revolution (1688) 6
Gordon, Alexander, smuggler of the Cabrach 106–8
Gordon, Alexander, 4th Duke of 52–3, 55
Gordon, Charles 108
Gordon, James, smuggler of the Cabrach 104
Gordon, James, Viscount Aboyne 86
Gordon, Janet 108
Gordon, John David, Laird of Beldornie 115

Gordon, Rev James 100, 102
Gordon, Robert, smuggler in Bordeaux 91
Gordon, William, smuggler of the Cabrach 104
Gordon Highlanders' Prisoners of War Fund
    (1917) 116–18
Gordon of Auchindoun, Adam 57, 77
Gordon of Auchmair, Alexander 114
Gordon of Bank, Jean 114
Gordon of Beldornie, George 81
Gordon of Beldornie, James 81
Gordon of Lesmoir, George 78, 85, 87
Gordon of Lesmoir, James 108
Gordon of Letterfourie, James 81–2
Gordon of Migvie, William 82
Gordon of Park, Adam 82
Gordon of Park, John 81
Gordon of Reekimlane, John 108
Gordon the Younger of Auchnacrie, Adam 82
Gow, Neil 67, 68
Grant, Major William 108
Grant of Rothiemurchus, Elizabeth 44–5
Granton, Charles Hope, Lord Justice Clerk 34
Greene, Graham 127
Guthrie, Rev Thomas 35, 37, 44

Haig, James (and Haig family) 24, 54
Harper's Manuel 58–9, 62
Harper's Weekly Gazette 51–2
Harthill and Edingarach, Leiths of 75, 81, 82
Henry, Robert, Doune excise officer 111–12
Her Majesty's Revenue & Customs (HMRC) 47,
    66, 126
Highland Boundary Fault (Highland Line') 37, 46
    raiding base of the Cabrach on 75–82
    regulations above and below 29–30, 31
Highland Land League 63, 65
Holcomb, Roscoe 70
Hudson, Steve 129–30
Hume, John R. 24
Hunter, Mollie 127–8
Huntly, Gordons of 75, 77, 78–9, 80, 81, 83, 84, 85,
    86–7, 90, 92, 93, 100–102, 104–5, 106

Ilay, Archibald Campbell, Earl of 16
illegality 2
Illicit Distillation (Scotland) Act (1822) 54–5
illicit distilling 8, 44, 62, 64, 66
    attitudes towards 34–5, 64
    Borders, large-scale productions in 24–5
    community operation 36
    economic benefits of 104–5
    factors encouraging 32–4
    prevalence of 53
    regret for passing of small stills 58
    ubiquitous nature of 45–6, 54–5
    see also Cabrach, barony and lands of the
Industrial Rvolution 121
Izzard, Eddie 130

Jacobite Rising (1715) 18
Jacobite Rising (1745) 18–19
Jacobite Rising (1688-89) 4
James, G.P.R. 127
James, Sid 127
James VI (I of England) 77, 79, 87
James VII (II of England) 4, 6, 90
James VIII (III of England, the 'Old Pretender')
    10–11
Jericho distillery, near Insch 123
Johnson, Dr Samuel 19
juniper 8

Kazee, Buell 69
Kennedy, Philip, smuggler in Collieston 97
Kilsyth, Battle of 83

Landseer, Sir Edwin 62
Lang, Fritz 127
legal system and policing framework in Scotland
    125–6
Leith, Alexander 82
Leith of Harthill, John 83
Leith of Harthill, Patrick 86
Lesmoir Castle 78, 83, 86
Liverpool, Robert Jenkinson, 2nd Earl of 51, 54
Lloyd George, David 116–18, 121
Lochnagar Distillery 57
Louis XV of France 100

Macdonald, Ian 63, 114
Macdonald of Strathpeffer, John 34
McGillewrich, Captain Patrick 77, 81
McGilligan, Robert, Gardenstown tidesman 113
McGoohan, Patrick 127

McIntosh, James, proprietor of Gordon Arms, Keith 118
McIntosh, Robert, merchant of the Cabrach 116
MacKendrick, Alexander 128
Mackenzie, Compton 128
McKenzie, Donald 104
Mackenzie, Sir Osgood 43
McKilligan, James, Provost of Banff 111
MacKinnon, Gillies 130
McNure, James, Doune excise officer 111–12
Malt Tax (1725) 10, 12, 14, 16, 18, 27, 92
    abolition of (1880) 63
    Glasgow riots against (1725) 92
malted barley, production of 7
Mar, 'Bobbing John,' Earl of 10–11
Memoirs of a Highland Lady (Grant, E.) 44–5
Miles, James, Don boatman 107–8
Milne, Robert, 'Hawker of Cloth' 114
Milne, Thomas, Doune excise officer 111–12
Mitchell, John 116–18
Monod, Paul 128
Montrose, James Graham, Marquis of 83, 86
Morewood, Samuel 46
Moss, Michael S. 24, 40
Munro, Captain Hugh 54
Murchison, Finlay 69

Napier, Lord Francis 64–5
Napier Commission of Enquiry (1883) 64–5
Napoleon Bonapatre 46
Napoleonic Wars 44, 51, 120

Parliamentary Committee on Distilleries, Stein's evidence to (1798) 32
Parliamentary Inquiry into Frauds Upon the Revenue (1736) 14
Peel, Sir Robert 59
Peterloo Massacre (1819) 51
Philiphaugh, Battle of 86
Pink, Kenneth 70
Pitt the Elder, William 30
Pitt the Younger, William 34, 47, 59
Plantation of Lewis 79–80
Pope Leo XII 100
Porteous, Captain John (Edinburgh City Guard) 14, 16–17, 27
Porteous Riot (1736) 14–15, 17–18

Prebble, John 9
Prendergast of Cadiz, Rosa Elena 115
Some Considerations on the Present State of Scotland (1744) 20–21
Prevention of Frauds by Private Distillers Act (1779) 26–7

Randall, Lieutenant Henry, R.N. 103, 106–7, 108
rapid distillation, development of 32
rationing, effect of 118–19
Redgrave, Michael 127
Rhynie-Mortlach 'highway betwixt Highlands and Lowlands' 77
Ritchie, Andrew, Peterhead coastguard 108
Robertson, Barry 87
Robertson, Stanley 67, 68
Robertson, Thomas 116
Robinson, F.J., 'Prosperity' (Viscount Goderich) 54
Robinson, George, Provost of Banff 109, 111
Ronald, William 116
Rose, William, factor to Lord Fife 112
Ross, William 81
Rosse, Rev James 86–7
Rouse, John, Don boatman 107–8

Scott, John (Edinburgh excise officer) 20
Scott, Sir Walter 14, 127
Scottish Excise Board 46, 93
    report on Cannonmills Distillery (1797) 32
Sillett, Stephen W. 5–6, 35, 43, 54, 85, 118
Sinclair, Sir John 36
Skinner, Rev John 68
Small Stills Act (1816) 46
Smith, Charlotte 127
Smith, Gavin 14
Smith, George (founder of Glenlivet distillery) 36, 55–7, 58
Smith, James 'Goshen,' gamekeeper to Beldornie 115–16
Smith, Richard, grocer in Aberdeen 106
smuggling
    attitudes towards 34–5, 64
    Banff, smuggler's royal burgh 109–13
    boldness of smugglers 106–8
    Campbeltown, example from 51–2
    droving and 40

expansion of 21–4, 25–6
General Assembly condemnation of 92
growth of, Bremner's perspective on 40–41
landowners' nervousness about 51
large-scale operation of 37
legendary nature of 37–40
necessity for survival 32
North-east coast, paradise for 96–7
Old Aberdeen, battle on streets of (1820) 104
origins of word 2
parliamentary debates about problem of 52–3
popular mythology about 41
reprisals by smugglers against legal distillation 57
universal nature of 14
whisky trade monopoly for smugglers 53–4
see also Cabrach, barony and lands of the
Smuggling Acts (1698, 1717, 1721 and 1745) 17
Soutar, Alastair 125
Speyside distilleries, Glenlivet and beginnings of 55–7
Spirits Act (1860) 62
Statistical Account of Scotland 32, 36, 44, 100
Stein, John (and Stein family) 24, 32
Stewart, Charles, tenant in the Cabrach 105
Stewart, Elizabeth 68
Stewart of Garth, Colonel David 31
Strathbogie 82, 83, 84, 115
Strathdon smuggling district 37, 41
Stuart, Charles Edward ('Young Pretender') 17–18
Stuart, Royal House of 83, 92
subsistence economy 9

taxation 16, 17–18, 47, 70, 116, 120, 122
Tayler, Alistair and Henrietta 112

Taylor, Duncan 123
Teaninich Distillery at Alness 54
Tennant of Auchenbay, John 50
Thorndike, Russell 127
Tibby Tamson o' the Buck 116–18
Tovey, Charles 62
Troy, Pat 70
Tucker, Thomas 2–3, 85

Union, Act of (1707) 2, 9–10, 16, 18, 90, 92, 96, 100, 120
Union of the Crowns (1603) 77
Usher, Andrew 62
Usher, Sir Robert 62

Wade, Major-General George 12, 15, 16
Wallace, Lord Thomas 53
Wallace, Paul 126
Wallace Commission 54
Walpole, Robert 16
whisky
    consumption of 12–13, 58–9, 62
    Dr Johnson's view on 19
    folklore about 67–71
    making of 7–8
    private distilling of 20
    production and demand for, expansion of 24–5
Wilkins, Francis 109, 110, 113
William and Mary 6
William Grant & Sons 8
William III 9, 29
William of Orange 4, 90
Willsher, George 123
Wilson, Ross 24–5